ROUNDUP

THE FLORENCE JAMES SERIES

The Plainsman
by Ken Mitchell

Roundup
by Barbara Sapergia

Saskatoon Pie
by Geoffrey Ursell

Talking Back
by Don Kerr

ROUNDUP

Barbara Sapergia

Coteau Books

This play is a work of fiction. Names, characters, places, and incidents either are the product of the author's imagination or are used fictitiously.

Edited by Geoffrey Ursell and Tom Bentley-Fisher.
Cover photograph courtesy of Saskatchewan Photographic Services (Photograph no. 82-819-52).
Cover design by Dik Campbell.
Book design by Val Jakubowski and Shelley Sopher.
Typeset by Val Jakubowski.
Printed and bound in Canada.

The publisher gratefully acknowledges the financial assistance of the Saskatchewan Arts Board and the Canada Council.

Canadian Cataloguing in Publication Data
Sapergia, Barbara, 1943-

Roundup

(Florence James series ; 2)
A play.

ISBN 1-50050-041-4

I. Title. II. Series.

PS8576.A641R6 1992 C812'.54 C92-098141-0
PR9199.3.S364R6 1992

COTEAU BOOKS
401 - 2206 Dewdney Avenue
Regina, Saskatchewan
Canada S4R 1H3

In memory of my uncle,
Ben Sapergia

FOREWORD

Much of Barbara Sapergia's writing is set in Saskatchewan, particularly in the rural community. In this work, we experience an enormous love and respect for the people of this province and for the uniqueness of life in this part of the world. She examines the difficulties and rewards inherent in trying to make a living in a vast rural community where isolation and hard economic times are everyday realities. She takes us to the heart of the prairies.

The struggle to make a living as a working farmer or rancher in this province is tremendous, with drought, high input costs, and low prices for agricultural products often leading to farm bankruptcy. The number of farm bankruptcies has never been higher. Families who have spent three or more generations working the land are suddenly faced with the reality of having to give up.

Roundup takes us into a world where politics no longer seems to provide the means to solutions, where struggling to do your utmost no longer seems to be good enough; its characters allow us to experience the originality of prairie people, and often contradict an outsider's expectations of them.

Roundup explores this world through the eyes of one family, the Petrescus, and particularly of one woman, Verna Petrescu. The questions Verna asks her husband and large extended family do not have simple answers, but we admire her courage in asking them. We admire the fact that she has the nerve to examine the possible advantages of letting go of the farm.

Verna Petrescu struggles with depression, anger, and self-doubt; her marriage is in danger of falling apart. Her husband, Paul, ignores the reality of his circumstances in order to survive on a day-to-day basis. And their daughter, Darcy, goes against the everyday wisdom that says she should leave the farm and, in so doing, risks her relationship with her mother.

Always though, Barbara Sapergia lets us experience this world through her sense of humour. And she never allows us to settle comfortably into one point of view.

The production of *Roundup* at Saskatoon's Twenty-Fifth Street Theatre incorporated a very realistic approach to the play. The set, designed by Michael Bantjes, demanded from the actors detailed task-oriented activity. An entire meal for ten people was actually made on stage, and much attention paid to the jobs required to be accomplished throughout the day of the roundup. This allowed little time for the characters to deal with the issues important to them. Rather, it forced the characters realistically to earn their way and to deal with their personal agendas through the relationships involved in completing the tasks at hand.

Roundup raises issues crucial to the future of people in Saskatchewan. History has bred in us the attitude that we must succeed against all odds. Although Barbara Sapergia taps into this kind of strength in her characters, she is not afraid of their weaknesses and vulnerabilities either. Succeeding against all odds is fine—but in order to achieve what? Her characters do not give up; they enter the future battered and bruised, but asking the questions and looking for the new adaptations which will ensure a positive way of life for a new generation of family farms in Saskatchewan.

The mandate of Twenty-Fifth Street Theatre is to develop and produce original Saskatchewan works, and clearly *Roundup* fits that mandate. I first became interested in the play in 1987, when I directed a workshop and staged reading at the Saskatchewan Playwrights Centre's Spring Festival of New Plays. My involvement continued as *Roundup* was workshopped and developed at Twenty-Fifth Street Theatre, prior to its premiere production, which I directed, as part of the Saskatchewan Playwrights Festival in 1990, featuring an all-Saskatchewan cast.

Barbara Sapergia is one of the most prolific writers in Saskatchewan, with numerous publications and dramatic productions during the past ten years, as well as a novel, *Foreigners*, a collection of poetry, and one of stories, *South Hill Girls*. Currently, she has a new play, based on the life of Canadian silent screen star Nell Shipman, in production at Twenty-Fifth Street Theatre.

TOM BENTLEY-FISHER
Artistic Director
Twenty-Fifth Street Theatre

PREFACE

Roundup was inspired by the droughts of the 1980s, but its foundations were laid long before. I grew up in the city of Moose Jaw, but spent as much time as I could visiting relatives who ran a cattle ranch in the hills near Old Wives Lake. It was a huge operation, eleven sections including leased pastured land, an extended family operation that supported not only my grandparents but several of their grown children and their families.

I was the city kid, fascinated by every aspect of country life, counting it a privilege to haul pails of water from the well, to help feed the chickens, and to at least try to sling hay bales around the way my cousins did. (This was before bales got so big you needed a front-end loader to sling them around.)

My cousins, who lived there all the time, and who were all too aware of the "fun" of doing chores, must have thought I was crazy, but they were amazingly tolerant, even when my ineptitude caused them pain, like the time I enthusiastically cranked the handle on the churn without noticing that my cousin Doris's thumb was in the way.

I suppose I romanticized a lot, but I still believe there were some wonderful things going on. The work was very hard, but there were school dances and community picnics, and skating on the slough. Neighbours did help each other. And I know I didn't just imagine that the horses and the hills and the grass were beautiful.

As a child, I saw the country life as timeless and unchanging. As an adult, I learned how economically fragile the life was and saw that it had already been changing back in the days when I helped my cousins gather eggs.

Crises in agriculture—and their reporting in the media—have become so common, and predictions of doom so frequent, that I fear many people have either stopped listening, or despaired that anything can be done to maintain the kind of people-centered rural life we used to have. So many farmers are gone, never to return.

A central paradox remains—in a hungry world, how is it that people who grow food have so little return for it, and so little control over their own destinies?

Roundup is not a documentary on "farm problems," or a recipe for "saving the family farm." It's a playwright's approach—an attempt to explore some of the many things, good and bad, that agriculture has meant to prairie people; and to look at what the "farm crisis" means to actual people. The characters are as real as my experience and imagination could make them.

A lot of people helped me with *Roundup*. The Saskatchewan Arts Board "bought me time" to work on it. The Saskatchewan Playwrights Centre workshopped the script, and Tom Bentley-Fisher of Twenty-Fifth Street Theatre worked with me throughout the year leading to production. Several fine dramaturges offered advice, including Frank Moher, Per Brask, and Michael Springate. John Juliani, Bill Valgardson, and Sandra Rabinovitch helped with the script for a one-hour version for CBC radio. Finally, and not least of all, friends and relatives on farms and ranches have given me time and patience and hospitality.

Roundup received its premiere production at Twenty-Fifth Street Theatre, Saskatoon, Saskatchewan from March 13 to April 8, 1990. The cast was as follows:

PAUL PETRESCU .... Mel Melymick
VERNA PETRESCU .... Marina Endicott
DARCY PETRESCU............... Burgandy Code
EILEEN DEACON .... Wendy Agnew
JESSIE GIBSON .... Ida Wasson
UNCLE POMPILIU............... Bill Hubbard
HARVEY FLINT .... Randy Hughson

DIRECTOR .... Tom Bentley-Fisher
SET DESIGN....................... Michael Bantjes
LIGHTING DESIGN.............. Bill McDermott
SOUND DESIGN.................. Ley Ward
STAGE MANAGER .... Laura Kennedy

CHARACTERS

PAUL PETRESCU: *A rancher in his late forties*

VERNA PETRESCU: *48, his wife*

DARCY PETRESCU: *17, their daughter*

EILEEN DEACON: *40, who lives on the neighbouring farm with her son, Greg*

JESSIE GIBSON: *70, a widowed neighbour of the Petrescus*

UNCLE POMPILIU LUPU: *71, Paul's uncle, a bachelor*

HARVEY FLINT: *A wealthy farmer and farm chemicals dealer*

SETTING

The setting is southwest Saskatchewan in the mid-eighties, somewhere west of Assiniboia. The Petrescus have a mixed farm; most of their land is rolling pasture suitable to ranching, although they also have some flat grain land where they plant wheat or other cereals.

The Petrescus and their neighbours have just come through several years of drought and poor prices. Many farms are failing, their neighbours leaving. Small towns falter and there's a fear that the old spirit of community in the countryside may be dying.

THE SET

The main playing area is a large country kitchen. It's fairly modern, part of a comfortable bungalow built about 1960. It is set back a few feet and raised a couple of feet above the stage, so that at the front we see its concrete foundation and in front of that, a smaller playing area, as wide as the stage but just a few feet deep. This area in front of the "house" has a gravel path and some rather dry grass and a few flowers. From the kitchen actors enter this area through the screen door (down left) and down a small set of steps. Other characters come in downstage right; they are coming up to the house from the corral where the roundup is taking place.

In the kitchen, up and right, is a door which leads to the root cellar. This area is set to the right of the kitchen and down a few steps, and angled away from the kitchen so it can seen clearly from all parts of the theatre. When this area is used, its lighting comes up while the kitchen lights go down.

A second door, up left, leads to the rest of the house—living-room and bedrooms—although we don't see any other rooms.

There is also a very small playing area to the left of the kitchen. It represents the area leading to the garden.

ACT ONE

The play begins in darkness. Sounds of a roundup: calves bawling, cows calling, dogs barking. Sounds fade as characters begin to speak.

Lights up on the kitchen. VERNA, EILEEN, *and* MRS. GIBSON *prepare food.* VERNA *checks her watch, then goes out the screen door and moves almost to centre stage. She looks down right, then calls out.*

VERNA: Darcy!

DARCY: *(Off)* Yeah.

VERNA: Are you coming up to the house?

DARCY: I'm busy right now.

VERNA: We could use you at the house.

DARCY: Mom, I can't just drop everything.

    PAUL *enters, down right.*

PAUL: What's your problem, Verna? Darcy's doin' a good job here.

VERNA: She's got one or two chores to do in the kitchen.

PAUL: Come off it. You got enough women up there to feed the whole municipality.

VERNA: I've got exactly two, and I'd like to see my own daughter lending a hand . . . . She's supposed to bake a cake.

PAUL: You just don't like her helpin' down here.

VERNA: That's not the point.

PAUL: Sure as hell is. You don't want her helpin' with the branding.

VERNA: All right, I don't.

    PAUL *moves in closer, so they don't have to talk quite so loud.*

PAUL: Why not?

VERNA: I just don't.

DARCY: *(Off)* Hey dad! Could you come over here?

PAUL: *(To* DARCY*)* Hang on a moment. *(To* VERNA*)* Try and relax. She's only doin' the vaccinations.

VERNA: Oh, sure.

PAUL: You know we don't let her do the castrating.

VERNA: You might as well.

PAUL: Why?

VERNA: She's determined to be one of the boys, no matter what it takes.

PAUL: Verna, it's hot as hell's armpit.

VERNA: Look, I didn't come down here to argue. I just want to know when you'll be finished.

PAUL: How do I know?

DARCY: *(Off)* Dad?

PAUL: Comin'.

VERNA: Oh, for heaven's sake. Try to carry on a conversation around here.

PAUL: We'll be done in about an hour—okay?

VERNA: Oh hell, take your time.

> VERNA *starts to walk to the house, but stops when she hears* DARCY *call out to* PAUL.

DARCY: *(Off)* Dad, there's a calf I think you should look at.

PAUL: No problem.

DARCY: Thanks . . . . I think Greg's got a cold beer for you.

PAUL: Sure, why not?

VERNA: Sure, why not. Take all bloody day if you want.

VERNA *strides up to the screen door (going around a cow pie in the middle of the path). She stops a moment to regain her cool.*

EILEEN *and* MRS. GIBSON, *who have been listening to the argument, begin talking, as though they haven't heard everything, while continuing to chop vegetables for a salad.*

EILEEN: If you're still having trouble with your pump, I could send Greg over after school Monday.

MRS. GIBSON: That's all right, Eileen, it's been taken care of.

VERNA *walks in.*

EILEEN: Oh, well that's good then. Verna, you're back.

EILEEN *and* MRS. GIBSON *stop chopping.*

MRS. GIBSON: So when do they want their supper?

VERNA: Oh, who knows?

VERNA *picks up a knife and starts chopping.*

EILEEN: Let's grab a quick coffee.

EILEEN *moves to a cupboard.*

VERNA: It's hot enough to fry your eyeballs, and you're gonna drink coffee?

MRS. GIBSON: Perhaps something a little stronger, eh girls? I've got a wee flask in my purse.

MRS. GIBSON *gets the whiskey as* EILEEN *pours coffee.*

EILEEN: Course, we'll never hear the end of it if one of the men comes up to the house.

VERNA: You think they haven't got a case of beer down at the corral?

MRS. GIBSON: Anyway, we'll just splash a little in our coffee, and nobody has to be the wiser.

EILEEN *and* MRS. GIBSON *prepare coffee.*

VERNA *keeps chopping.*

EILEEN: Verna?

VERNA: You go ahead.

EILEEN: Verna . . .

VERNA: I just want to be ready.

EILEEN: Be a martyr then. *(Raises her cup to* MRS. GIBSON*)* Well, here's lookin' at you, kid.

EILEEN *and* MRS. GIBSON *clink their cups together.*

MRS. GIBSON: To good times and good friends . . . . Oh, I had a letter from Cathy Flowers the other day.

EILEEN: So how do they like Edmonton?

MRS. GIBSON: I think they still miss the farm. Frank says it's an easy place to drive a cab though.

EILEEN: Oh yeah—all the streets have numbers instead of names.

MRS. GIBSON: I've always preferred names myself somehow.

EILEEN: They could've hung on another year, damn it. *(*VERNA *starts to chop harder)* Verna? *(*VERNA *doesn't hear)* Verna.

VERNA: What?

EILEEN: Do you have to chop quite so hard?

VERNA: *(Stops)* No, I guess I don't.

EILEEN: So you and Paul had a little fight. Don't take it so hard.

VERNA: We did not have a "fight."

MRS. GIBSON: Gibson and I had a grand fight once. I was churning butter, and I grabbed the handle and yanked it around like it was his arm I was tearing out.

EILEEN: That's one way to get your chores done.

MRS. GIBSON: Only I didn't see Gibson had his thumb in the way. Oh God, you should have seen his eyes. But he wouldn't say a word. His thumb turned black and blue. It's a wonder it didn't drop off.

EILEEN: I used to like watching you two when I was little. Always stealing a kiss when you thought nobody was looking.

MRS. GIBSON: Ah, Gibson was a lovely man in that way. That's the hardest part, you know.

VERNA *finishes the salad, and starts to work rolling cabbage rolls.*

EILEEN: You still miss it?

MRS. GIBSON: You mean, because I'm seventy-five? Age doesn't enter into it, Eileen.

EILEEN: Well, that's good to hear. Eh, Verna? (VERNA *keeps working.*) Verna, what are you doing now?

VERNA: Finishing off the cabbage rolls.

EILEEN: We've already got enough to feed the entire Romanian army.

MRS. GIBSON: And each one of them a work of art.

EILEEN: When Verna rolls a cabbage leaf, it stays rolled.

VERNA *just keeps working.*

UNCLE POMPILIU *enters down right (from the corral) and steps in the middle of the cow pie without noticing. He enters the kitchen, letting the screen door slam.*

POMPILIU: Well, well, isn't this nice? Ah, what it is to be a woman and live soft.

EILEEN: Mr. Lupu. You're tracking cow manure all over Verna's clean floor.

POMPILIU: *Doamne! (Looks at his feet)* I'll wipe them right away. (*With elaborate care, he wipes his shoes on the mat by the door.*) There. Clean as a whistle.

MRS. GIBSON: Would you like a cup of coffee, Mr. Lupu?

POMPILIU: A cup of coffee, is it? Hmmnn.

EILEEN *gets a cup from the cupboard.*

EILEEN: Maybe we could liven it up a little.

MRS. GIBSON: A little . . . Scottish coffee?

POMPILIU: *(Sees bottle)* Ah. Well yes, my old bones could stand a little of that.

EILEEN: Old bones.

POMPILIU: I'll be seventy-one years in the spring, young lady. Show a little respect.

EILEEN: You don't know what you're asking.

EILEEN *laughs. In spite of herself,* VERNA *is amused.*

MRS. GIBSON *offers the whiskeyed coffee.*

MRS. GIBSON: There you are, Mr. Lupu.

POMPILIU: There I am indeed, dear lady. *Buna sanatate.(Sips)* Oh, that's beautiful. Like the home-brew my dad used to make—my it was good.

MRS. GIBSON: Helped pay the bills too, I don't wonder.

POMPILIU: Oh yes. Some years we did better on the whiskey than we did on the crop. *(They laugh)* Verna, what are you doing? Come and sit with your friends.

EILEEN: Yeah, Verna—come on.

VERNA: I have to finish these cabbage rolls.

POMPILIU: Sit. I'll do it.

VERNA: What about your old bones?

POMPILIU: Jessie's whiskey has warmed them up. Now sit. Drink some coffee. Have a little whiskey.

EILEEN *goes to get a cup.*

VERNA: I don't want any.

EILEEN *stops.*

MRS. GIBSON: Verna?

VERNA: I'm just trying to get the work done.

EILEEN *looks around for a distraction. She sees the salad.*

EILEEN: You have any new peas yet?

EILEEN *goes to a cupboard, gets two bowls.*

VERNA: We're not gonna start cooking peas.

EILEEN: Who said we were? We'll just shell them and throw them in the salad.

VERNA: Raw?

EILEEN: Sure. Don't you remember eating them in the garden when you were a kid?

POMPILIU: Eileen is right, it'll give the salad that extra little something.

VERNA: But—

MRS. GIBSON: Verna, everything is under control.

POMPILIU: You need a little change of scene.

VERNA: Change of scene—hah!

POMPILIU: Go.

VERNA: Oh, all right.

Bowls in hand, they go out the screen door, down the step and through the garden gate, voices trailing away as they go.

Say, there is a bit of a breeze out here.

EILEEN: Of course there is.

POMPILIU: Young people. *Asha.*

MRS. GIBSON: They do take things seriously, don't they?

POMPILIU: They should relax a little, eh? Like us.

MRS. GIBSON: Oh yes—like us.

POMPILIU: Now don't start in on a poor old man.

MRS. GIBSON: Poor old man.

POMPILIU: Hey, we should have some *placinta* with this.

POMPILIU *goes to the kitchen counter and rummages around.*

MRS. GIBSON: Are you trying to change the subject?

POMPILIU: I know Verna made some with raisins.

In a biscuit tin he finds some placinta (a Romanian pastry).

MRS. GIBSON: It's quite a simple question, you know.

POMPILIU *brings the tin to the table.*

POMPILIU: There we are, Jessie. This will keep our strength up.

MRS. GIBSON: Good, I can see we're going to need it.

POMPILIU: Yes, now I've been thinking, dear lady. There is very good movie on in Assiniboia tonight. I think we should be there.

MRS. GIBSON: I don't know. I should stay and help Verna clean up.

POMPILIU: She has Eileen and Darcy. They never miss us. We just wait till they get talking about cattle prices, then we slip right out the door.

MRS. GIBSON: Ah, Mr. Lupu, you're a naughty fellow.

POMPILIU: I suppose so. But the way I figure, I'm getting into my golden years, eh?

MRS. GIBSON: That's one way of describing them.

POMPILIU: My golden years, yes. And I want to have a little fun.

MRS. GIBSON: I've never been against a little fun. However, it's time we came to a decision.

They hear the voices of VERNA *and* EILEEN *returning.*

VERNA: *(Off)* I think we've got enough.

POMPILIU: *Doamne,* I said I'd do the cabbage rolls.

MRS. GIBSON: I guess you'd better then.

He jumps up and starts to work.

MRS. GIBSON *stands near the window and listens.*

Lights go down on the kitchen as EILEEN *and* VERNA *come up to the house and sit on the front steps to shell peas.* EILEEN *pops a few in her mouth.*

EILEEN: Just how long do you plan on keeping this up?

VERNA: I'm not keeping anything up.

EILEEN: Like hell. You're in a world-class snit.

VERNA: I'm not in a "snit." And mind your own business.

EILEEN: No, I won't. You and Paul have had a good life on this place.

VERNA: That's your opinion.

EILEEN: I mean, can you really think of doing anything else?

VERNA: Yes, I most certainly can.

EILEEN: Have you ever thought about talking to someone? Getting some counselling?

VERNA: Are you out of your mind? I'm not telling my private affairs to some stranger.

EILEEN: Do you think they care? Verna, they've heard it all before.

VERNA: Not from me they haven't.

EILEEN: Honestly, sometimes you sound just like your mother.

VERNA: You take that back.

EILEEN: All right, I take it back . . . . Darcy dropped by to visit the other day—

VERNA: Darcy! Don't get me started on Darcy. *(Gets up)*

EILEEN: We had a little talk over coffee. (VERNA *doesn't stop.*) Never mind.

They go back in, EILEEN *bringing the peas. Lights up on the kitchen and* POMPILIU, *still working on cabbage rolls.*

MRS. GIBSON *moves away from the window to the table.* EILEEN *puts the peas in the salad, mixes them in.* VERNA *tries to take over again making cabbage rolls.*

POMPILIU: Have a little of that coffee now, Verna. I'm doing this.

VERNA: Oh, all right.

MRS. GIBSON: *(Pouring coffee)* with the whiskey?

VERNA: Why not?

MRS. GIBSON: *(Adds shot of whiskey and hands cup to* VERNA*)* There. That'll bring back memories.

EILEEN: You mean from the days of home-brew?

MRS. GIBSON: Aye. Dan and Trandafira had a still in the spare bedroom when Verna and Paul got married.

EILEEN: You're kidding.

POMPILIU: They had to move it out so Paul and Verna could sleep there. Oh, I tell you, the smell.

MRS. GIBSON: And there's Verna, nice English girl, daughter of the United Church minister, on her honeymoon in a still.

VERNA: I never did tell Mother about that one.

POMPILIU: Nice lady, but she thinks only English people know how to do things.

MRS. GIBSON: She was a bit of a stuffed shirtwaist—no offense, Verna.

(Laughter)

VERNA: She never set foot on this place. Not once.

EILEEN: That's sad. She never got to see how beautiful it is.

VERNA: She wouldn't have thought so.

POMPILIU: Your daddy came to visit, though. They were afraid to offer him a drink, because he was an English priest.

VERNA: A minister, Uncle Pompiliu.

POMPILIU: So I'd take him out on the porch, and we'd have a quiet little sip together.

VERNA: I never knew that.

POMPILIU: The day we know everything, my girl, we might as well curl up and die.

VERNA: What's that? Some old Romanian proverb?

POMPILIU: No, I just made it up.

VERNA *smiles.*

MRS. GIBSON: You have to admit, Verna, we had some good times in this house. People would just drop over in the evening.

POMPILIU: Dan would take down his fiddle . . . and the boys would push the furniture against the wall—

MRS. GIBSON: And how we danced.

POMPILIU: Oh yes, Jessie could cut quite a rug in those days.

MRS. GIBSON: In those days!

MRS. GIBSON: And Verna—the dresses Paul's mother made. You told her what you wanted—or drew a little picture—and in a few hours, she'd come back with your dress, just the way you dreamed it.

POMPILIU: I seem to remember you in something red.

MRS. GIBSON: You mean my crimson taffeta? With the gathered skirt and three rows of ruffles around the hem?

POMPILIU: That must be the one.

MRS. GIBSON: Oh, and your wedding dress, Verna. That was Trandafira's finest work.

VERNA: Not that many people got to see it.

MRS. GIBSON: I was there. I saw it.

They hear DARCY'S *step outside, and* VERNA *is brought back to the present and her annoyance with* PAUL *and* DARCY. DARCY *comes in, closing the screen door gently.*

VERNA *jumps up, goes to the fridge and gets out mayonnaise for the salad.*

DARCY: Hi.

EILEEN: Hi, Darcy. We were just talking about your mom and dad's wedding.

VERNA: It's about time, Darcy.

DARCY *ignores* VERNA. *Annoyed,* VERNA *rummages in a cupboard for things to put in the salad dressing.*

DARCY *washes her hands and starts getting out pans, ingredients, etc.*

EILEEN: *(To* DARCY*)* What are you making?

DARCY: Spice cake. Greg really likes them.

EILEEN: True love, eh? He'll never starve while she's around.

VERNA: Starve? Hell, he'll never go without dessert.

EILEEN: *(To* DARCY*)* Did you get that saddle you and Greg went to look at the other day?

DARCY: No . . . I didn't.

VERNA: Saddle?

Seeing DARCY *looking embarrassed and* VERNA *puzzled,* UNCLE POMPILIU *seizes the moment for a diversion. He puts the cabbage rolls on the stove to simmer.*

POMPILIU: Well, dear ladies, I'll see what's doing at the corral.

EILEEN: Hey, don't let Darcy scare you off.

POMPILIU: Don't you worry about old Uncle Pompiliu. I do okay.

He walks toward the door.

EILEEN: Well, we knew that. *(Laughs)*

POMPILIU *goes out, slamming the screen door. He walks down the path, through the cow pie, and exits down right (to corral).*

DARCY: I bet Uncle Pompiliu has always done okay.

EILEEN: He sure sold his land at the right moment.

DARCY: And got that apartment in Assiniboia.

EILEEN: Not bad for an old codger.

MRS. GIBSON: Old codger!

EILEEN: Oops, sorry, Mrs. Gibson. It's just that I've always thought of Mr. Lupu as a codger.

VERNA: I nearly died when he got the Ferrari.

MRS. GIBSON: I didn't even know what a Ferrari was until he took me for a spin in it.

VERNA: Aha! So he's taken you out in the Ferrari.

MRS. GIBSON: Aye. As I said. For a wee spin. It goes like the wind, Verna.

EILEEN: I bet it does. *(Laughter)*

DARCY: So you guys were talking about Mom and Dad's wedding?

VERNA: No.

MRS. GIBSON: I was there, you know, Darcy. Gibson and I stood up with them. Paul and Verna were nervous enough, but Reverend Postle was shaking like an aspen.

EILEEN: Why? What happened?

VERNA: Nothing. It's ancient history.

> EILEEN *looks at her expectantly.*

It's just . . . I'd wanted Dad to marry us, but he didn't dare because of Mother.

EILEEN: And? And?

VERNA: Dad set it up with the Methodist minister.

EILEEN: And he was afraid she'd find out?

VERNA: Mother thought I was going to a strawberry social . . . . *(remembers)* She was furious when we told her. She stormed over to Reverend Postle's house and told him he was no Christian.

MRS. GIBSON: That sounds like Minnie, all right. She never spoke to me again.

DARCY: *(To* VERNA*)* Tell about Grandma making your dress.

VERNA: We've done dresses already.

EILEEN: Aw, come on.

VERNA: There's nothing to tell. She made me a dress. Period.

DARCY: There is too. It's a wonderful dress. Long sleeves, big full skirt. And Grandma embroidered it with flowers all around the neckline.

MRS. GIBSON: Oh, Verna, you looked so beautiful in it.

EILEEN: It sounds lovely.

VERNA: It was.

DARCY: Maybe I'll wear it when I get married.

VERNA: We'll see about that when the time comes.

DARCY: All right, we will.

VERNA: Just get on with your work.

EILEEN: Those were good times.

VERNA: There was a damn sight more work.

EILEEN: But I always liked the things we used—wood stoves, cream separators—

MRS. GIBSON: Don't talk to me of cream separators. I never want to see one again.

EILEEN: They were the devil to wash, all right. But sometimes I can still almost see it in the corner of the kitchen where mom used to keep it.

MRS. GIBSON: The ghost of the cream separator. *(Laughs)*

DARCY: I wish I could've lived on the farm then. You fell in love, got married, and got right down to work.

VERNA: That's romantic garbage.

MRS. GIBSON: People did have to work awfully hard, Darcy. I think it wore the men out too young.

VERNA: That's right.

MRS. GIBSON: Perhaps there was a spirit to it that's gone.

DARCY: That's what I mean—the spirit.

VERNA: Oh, for heaven's sake.

DARCY: No, I'm right. People knew how to be heroes then.

VERNA: You think it doesn't take heroes to survive on the farm nowadays?

DARCY: But it was different. Eileen knows what I mean.

VERNA: Oh?

DARCY: What about Uncle Pete? Dad says he walked home in a blizzard once. Twenty miles of railroad track, and all he could see was the bit of track in front of his feet. Twenty miles! Just to get home to Auntie Sofie.

VERNA: The damn fool. Auntie Sofie would've been just fine on her own.

DARCY: Oh, Mom. You told me about it yourself. You used to tell the best stories. (VERNA *ignores her.*) Tell them about when the horse ran away with Auntie Esther.

VERNA: I'm sure they've heard it a thousand times before.

EILEEN: I don't think I have.

DARCY: Come on, Mom.

EILEEN: Yeah, Verna.

DARCY: See, Auntie Esther was about ten. Dad and the other kids were younger. She had to drive them to school in a democrat. And they had this horse, Snake—

VERNA: We really haven't got time for this.

DARCY: Snake was this real ornery horse, and either he wouldn't go at all, or he'd go like crazy—

VERNA: Darcy, can't you just get your cake in the oven and be done with it.

DARCY: Anyway, Eileen, they were driving home from school one day and they just left the school yard when something made Snake shy—

MRS. GIBSON: It was a gopher ran right across his path. And that old Snake just takes off like a flash of lightning. Well, Esther drops the reins, and the little ones are shrieking and crying, and the democrat's hitting every gopher and badger hole and just about flying apart, and—

EILEEN: Wait a minute. You weren't in school then, Mrs. Gibson.

MRS. GIBSON: I saw it all from my window.

VERNA: Did you?

MRS. GIBSON: And the handsome young schoolteacher runs for his horse. He takes one great leap onto its back and goes galloping after them. He comes up beside the buggy—just like you see in the movies—and he leans over and grabs the reins, and stops that Snake in his tracks.

DARCY: See, Mom! Talk about heroes.

MRS. GIBSON: Yes, indeed.

EILEEN: He must have been some rider.

MRS. GIBSON: An excellent horseman. Oh, he was a bonny man.

> EILEEN *and* VERNA *exchange a look.*

DARCY: How well did you know this "bonny man"?

MRS. GIBSON: Very well. Mr. Grey-Owen boarded with Gibson and me.

EILEEN: Aha!

MRS. GIBSON: Don't you "aha" me, young lady. There was nothing that went on that shouldn't have. Mind you, I didn't have him back a second year—that might've been pushing things.

VERNA: You don't say.

MRS. GIBSON: Thought you knew all the old stories, did you?

> VERNA *doesn't answer.*

EILEEN: What did he look like, this teacher?

MRS. GIBSON: Ah, he had lovely dark hair and soft grey eyes, and his Christian name was Gabriel.

DARCY: Oh, Mrs. Gibson. He sounds really cute.

MRS. GIBSON: Cute! Hah! He was handsome, I tell you.

EILEEN: I wonder what became of him.

MRS. GIBSON: I wonder.

DARCY: There was a different spirit to life. Things were simpler then.

VERNA: Oh yes. It was simpler, all right. Life's a lot simpler when you don't know what's going on in the world. When you don't have any schooling past grade eight. When you don't have any choices—

EILEEN: There was more to it than that. When Dan and Trandafira's barn burned down, people came from miles around to help.

VERNA: Okay. These things happened all right. But they weren't the whole story. Not by a long shot.

EILEEN: Well, of course not—

VERNA: I can name you four women in our school district who lost babies because they couldn't get to town in the winter.

EILEEN: People lose babies in the city too.

VERNA: Not because they live thirty miles from a hospital. Oh, and then there's Arnie Chisholm. Got dragged by a horse at Thorntons' roundup. Broke his hip and pelvis and never walked again. Oh yes, I'd say it was hard on the men.

EILEEN: Verna, what is eating you?

VERNA: Just don't tell me about the good old days on the farm. Darcy wants to spend her life trying to bring them back. And you two—you sit there egging her on. Well, I want her to see the other side.

DARCY: I do see the other side.

EILEEN: She does, Verna.

VERNA: Oh sure she does. "People fell in love and got married." Well, not all those couples lived happily ever after. Or maybe you've forgotten how Ralph Aiken used to beat his wife.

EILEEN: I haven't forgotten.

VERNA: He treated her and those kids worse than animals. Arlee Aiken never left that farm one whole long winter.

EILEEN: Verna, don't.

VERNA: And nobody wanted to know. She finally figured out there was no way she'd get out of there alive.

EILEEN: All right! We should have helped her. But you can't blame it on the farm.

VERNA: No? You're all telling me how good it was. I'm just setting the record straight.

EILEEN: You're setting it crooked.

VERNA: Oh, and remember, Darcy, the night Bailey Wright came over to tell us about the voices he heard coming up through the snowbanks?

DARCY: So? You think they don't have weirdos in the city?

VERNA: He was so damn pleased he'd finally figured out how to shut them up—by sticking wadded-up toilet paper in his ears.

DARCY: Mom, stop, this is gross.

VERNA: His teeth were all crusted with food and his beard looked like a magpie's nest. You remember, all right.

DARCY: You're not being fair.

VERNA: Fair! We work here all our lives, we take the cold and the loneliness and the boredom—

DARCY: No! It's not like that.

VERNA: Isn't it? Well then, you tell me.

DARCY: Well . . . . It's work that changes from season to season. You get to try new things. You get to be your own boss.

VERNA: That's a laugh. The bank's your boss.

DARCY: And there's more room . . . to move around in. You can hear yourself think . . . and I get to work with Dad and learn the stuff he knows. And the air's clean, not like the city—

VERNA: Sure. We get to breath herbicides instead of traffic fumes.

DARCY: You twist everything I say. I know it's not perfect. But I look outside . . . and that's what I want to see when I'm working. Don't you know what I mean? It's grass and hills and sky, as far as you can see. Mom, it's beautiful here.

VERNA: Oh yes. There's the other great myth. Our problems all fade away when we see a wheat field blowing in the breeze.

EILEEN: She didn't say that.

VERNA: Darcy, we can sit here until the banks take away all our land. Nobody'll even notice. And I will not be bought off by a few prairie sunsets.

EILEEN: Verna, will you take it easy.

VERNA: No, I will not. I married Paul, and that's fine, but I should have done what I wanted first. I was going to go to normal school and train for a teacher, and I just threw it all away. Now Darcy wants to do the same, and I'm not letting her.

DARCY: You're not letting me!

EILEEN: Verna—

VERNA: Because it doesn't work. It just doesn't.

(*Starting to cry,* VERNA *moves to the cellar door.*)

DARCY: Where are you going?

VERNA: I have to get some stuff from the cellar.

DARCY: Wait—I'll help you.

VERNA *goes down to the cellar, followed by* DARCY.

MRS. GIBSON: Well . . . I don't think I've had a chance to ask how you're keeping.

EILEEN: I'm all right. I've got Greg to worry about. And money, and politics. And I'm on a committee at the church.

MRS. GIBSON: Filling up the time?

EILEEN: I guess . . . I get lonely sometimes.

Lights down slightly in the kitchen and up on the cellar as VERNA *and* DARCY *come downstairs.*

VERNA *immediately starts checking the shelves, not wanting to pursue the argument.*

VERNA: Well, at least it's cool down here. That does feel good. Where's the corn relish?

DARCY: In the corner.

VERNA *spots it and goes to get one.*

VERNA: Darcy, do you see any of that sauerkraut from Auntie Esther? I was sure I had a couple of jars left.

DARCY: I'll get it.

DARCY *climbs on a stool, finds a pint sealer of sauerkraut, and hands it down to* VERNA.

VERNA: While you're up there, get some of that tomato ketchup from Mrs. Gibson.

DARCY: Okay.

DARCY *finds the ketchup, hands it down, and jumps down from stool.*

VERNA: She does a real nice job on it, doesn't she? I think she puts in a little brown sugar. Ketchup needs to be a bit sweet, don't you think?

DARCY: I suppose it does.

VERNA: I've tried to get that recipe out of her for years, but she never will tell.

DARCY: She told me it came from Gibson's mother. She had to promise to keep it a secret. Mom . . . .

VERNA: Really? She never mentioned that to me.

VERNA *looks around to see what else she could take upstairs.*

DARCY: Why can't it work? (VERNA *ignores question*) Mom, why can't it? (VERNA *sees something on another shelf.*) If I can grow food, I should be able to sell it to somebody who needs it.

VERNA *continues to ignore her.*

DARCY: We can make it work, that's what I believe . . . . Mom, talk to me.

VERNA: Don't you understand? What we want doesn't count.

DARCY: It must count.

VERNA: Are you forgetting we haven't had a decent rain around here for three years?

DARCY: It's gonna rain again.

VERNA: The pastures are burned up.

DARCY: The pastures will come back.

VERNA: What about the people? Will the people come back?

DARCY: This is my life.

VERNA: It isn't anybody's life. Not any more.

DARCY: There's something I want to tell you.

VERNA: Don't you talk to me about getting married.

VERNA *looks at the jars, silently counting them.*

DARCY: Mom, for Pete's sake!

VERNA: *(Startled)* What?

DARCY: I'm trying to talk to you—

VERNA: Fine. Just don't talk to me about you and Greg getting married.

DARCY: Mom—

VERNA: You are too young, and you haven't even finished high school. Next topic.

DARCY: All right . . . . You and Dad.

VERNA: Just leave it alone, Darcy.

DARCY: I wish you could see yourself. I wish you could hear the things you say.

VERNA: You don't understand. You haven't lived here for the last thirty years.

DARCY: So explain it to me. I don't see anything Dad's done that's so awful.

VERNA: You wouldn't. You always take his side.

DARCY: I'm not on any side. This is my family I'm talking about.

VERNA: You don't know anything about it. You think life's some kind of fairy tale—like you just get married and everything is taken care of.

DARCY: What are you saying? . . . . Don't you love him any more?

VERNA is caught off-guard. She wants to answer "yes," but can't quite say it.

VERNA: Don't be ridiculous. Look, we have to go up.

DARCY: Yeah . . . . There's something I wanted to tell you.

VERNA: All right, what is it?

VERNA is finally listening, but DARCY loses her nerve.

DARCY: Never mind . . . it'll keep.

DARCY starts to gather up the jars they have chosen. She sees a jar on a shelf, which she hadn't noticed earlier.

Oh, let's take a currant jelly.

She grabs a jar and hands it to VERNA. VERNA reaches for the jar, but it slips through her fingers, falls to the floor, and breaks.

VERNA: Damn!

Lights fade on the cellar and come up on the kitchen. EILEEN and MRS. GIBSON hear the jar break.

VERNA and DARCY enter from the cellar and start putting jars on counter.

EILEEN: What happened, Verna? Did you throw one of those at Darcy?

VERNA: I'd say mind your own business, but it wouldn't be any use, would it?

EILEEN: Nope.

As they speak, PAUL enters down right and walks up to the house. He comes through the screen door. VERNA looks at him, then turns to open a jar of pickles.

MRS. GIBSON: Hello, Paul.

PAUL: Hi, Mrs. Gibson. Eileen.

PAUL looks at VERNA, then goes to the table and sits down. He looks around expectantly. DARCY notices.

DARCY: Coffee, dad?

PAUL: Actually, a beer would go great.

DARCY brings a beer from the fridge.

VERNA looks annoyed.

PAUL: Thanks, Darcy.

PAUL tips it back and drains half of it in one gulp. VERNA tries not to watch. He sees the placinta UNCLE POMPILIU got out, which no one has eaten.

Say, is anyone eating this *placinta?*

PAUL tucks into it, leaving a big pile of crumbs in his wake. Without any conscious thought, DARCY comes and wipes them up.

VERNA: Did you come up for anything in particular, Paul?

PAUL: *(Sips)* Just thought I'd see if Darcy'd finished up here.

VERNA: What? You don't need her.

PAUL: Actually, we do.

VERNA: You're almost done for the day.

PAUL: Doesn't matter.

He tips back his beer and gulps the rest of it. VERNA looks angry. DARCY picks up the bottle and takes it over to the sink counter.

VERNA: Oh, for heaven's sake.

DARCY: I won't be long, Mom. Let's just get it done.

VERNA: Oh, all right. Get out. Both of you.

DARCY: See ya soon.

> PAUL *and* DARCY *go out.* VERNA *grabs the door before it slams, and follows them out.*

VERNA: Paul. Wait a minute.

PAUL: *(To* DARCY*)* You go ahead to the corral.

DARCY: All right. *(*DARCY *goes)*

PAUL: So, Verna, what is it?

VERNA: How many calves do you have left, anyway?

PAUL: Oh, couple of dozen.

VERNA: What on earth do you need Darcy for?

PAUL: We just like having her around. Tell you the truth, things seem to go that little bit better when she's there.

VERNA: Paul, this is the last time I'm letting her work outside at the roundup. You do not need her.

PAUL: Neither do you.

VERNA: I certainly do. We've got a lot of work to do.

PAUL: You got all those women in there—

VERNA: Women! That's right. Women. Who else ever does anything in the kitchen?

PAUL: Would you give me a break? I'm workin' at the corral.

> PAUL *moves off toward the corral (down right).* VERNA *follows him.*

VERNA: Oh sure. And you come up to the kitchen, and you plunk yourself down like . . . like you owned the place.

> PAUL *stops.*

PAUL: But I do.

VERNA: Like it was God's will for you to sit there . . . like a great big lump . . . and have Darcy and me look after you.

PAUL: I never said you had to, did I?

VERNA: You expect it.

PAUL: For Pete's sake, I do not.

VERNA: I can see it in your body, your face—

PAUL: My face. Now even my face is wrong?

VERNA: It's . . . your attitude. That's what I can't stand.

PAUL: I don't have any attitude.

VERNA: Like you just have to wait around . . . and everything'll be taken care of.

PAUL: I just . . . try to be myself. I mean, a guy has to have . . . confidence.

VERNA: Paul, have you ever in your life picked up a dishrag and wiped the crumbs off a table?

PAUL: What's that got to do with anything? I do all the outside work.

VERNA: What about harvest?

PAUL: What about it?

VERNA: When harvest comes I do plenty. I drive the tractor. I haul grain to the elevator.

PAUL: Well, sure—it's our busiest time. The work's gotta get done.

VERNA: The work's gotta get done. Of course.

PAUL: All the women do it, Vern. You know they do.

VERNA: How come nobody worries about what's women's work then?

PAUL: Why should they? We're all in it together, aren't we?

VERNA: How come we're not all in it together in the house?

PAUL: But that's different.

VERNA: Is it?

PAUL: What are we talking about? You want me to wipe the table sometimes? Is that it?

VERNA: Do you have to be so bloody literal?

PAUL: Do you want me to or not?

VERNA: All right, yes! I would like it if you sometimes just picked up the dishcloth and wiped off the goddamn table.

PAUL: Why should I?

VERNA: Out of consideration, that's why. Because they're your crumbs too. Because "we're all in this together."

PAUL: For Pete's sake, Verna. Is this what's eating you?

VERNA: Oh, don't be so stupid.

PAUL: Well, is it?

VERNA: It's part of it.

PAUL: Is it just wiping the table, or would there be other things?

VERNA: Wiping the table is an example.

PAUL: How often would I have to do it?

VERNA: If you have to ask, it's not going to work.

PAUL: Look, I better get back to the corral. *(Starts to go)*

VERNA: That's right, run away as soon as we start to get somewhere.

PAUL: I'm not running away. I just wanna get the job finished. Okay?

VERNA: I give up. *(Turns back to house)*

PAUL: *(Moves off)* We'll talk about it later.

VERNA: Forget it.

> VERNA *slams into the house.* PAUL *goes off (to the corral).*

Hell.

> *She grabs a dishrag, wipes counters furiously.*

MRS. GIBSON: Now, now, Verna.

VERNA: Dammit all, I'm forty-eight years old, and I'm getting a little bit tired.

MRS. GIBSON: Tell me about it.

VERNA: Men! I'm sick of it. Feeding them. Looking after their cuts and bruises. Their feelings.

EILEEN: Oh, come on. It's not that bad.

VERNA: Who says it isn't?

MRS. GIBSON: It's true Trandafira raised those boys to think the sun rose and set around them. I think she was trying to make up for all the hard work they had to do.

VERNA: The women worked hard. Who made it up to them?

MRS. GIBSON: I don't know.

VERNA: Why do the men always have the edge?

EILEEN: They don't.

VERNA: Yes, they do. And do you want to know why?

EILEEN: I'm sure you're going to tell me.

VERNA: Because they're a bit stronger, that's why.

MRS. GIBSON: A bit?

VERNA: And they think that makes them better. They find some woman to make a home for them, to do chores for them, to have babies for them. But they never think our work is quite as important as theirs.

MRS. GIBSON: When you're together late at night, does it really matter?

VERNA: Yes it does, damn it. It does matter. I'm not a servant.

EILEEN: Things can't have been that bad. You did manage to have Darcy.

MRS. GIBSON: Paul must have said the right thing once or twice.

EILEEN *and* MRS. GIBSON *laugh.*

VERNA: Don't you make fun of me. I want to be partners. Equal partners.

EILEEN: Okay, okay. But look—at least everything will be different for Darcy.

VERNA: What do you mean?

EILEEN: She doesn't see any difference between men's work and women's. She'll do anything.

VERNA: You think that makes her liberated or something?

EILEEN: Well, doesn't it?

VERNA: That's not liberation, it's voluntary slavery.

EILEEN: Oh, bull.

VERNA: It's her version of the Total Woman—the Good Farm Wife. She runs the house, she raises the babies. She works in the community, the church, the Wheat Pool.

MRS. GIBSON: What's wrong with that?

VERNA: Then in her spare time, she gets out on the land. She ploughs, she seeds, she harrows. She feeds the stock, she fixes fence, she cleans the barn . . . she shovels shit.

EILEEN: What's wrong with that?

VERNA: And she even works the roundup. She vaccinates, brands, ear-marks, de-horns and castrates the calves—just like the men. And then!

EILEEN: Would you give us a break?

VERNA: And then she runs up to the house, throws on a freshly ironed dress, and pops a spice cake in the oven. As her weary man plods up to the house, she greets him with a kiss and shoves a cold beer into his hands!

They look at her for a moment.

MRS. GIBSON: Well. Are you quite finished?

VERNA: Not by a long shot.

EILEEN: Okay, I see what you're saying.

VERNA: No you don't.

EILEEN: But maybe Darcy's just doing what you always wanted to do.

VERNA: No way. We didn't do those things when I was a girl. And we didn't want to.

EILEEN: I think you're jealous of her.

VERNA: I'm not jealous! But she thinks she's bloody Superwoman.

MRS. GIBSON: Nonsense. She's only trying to be grown-up.

VERNA: What?

MRS. GIBSON: And she tries to look confident because she's scared inside.

VERNA: Scared? Darcy?

MRS. GIBSON: And the other thing you're forgetting is, it's her life. Until you get that into your skull, you're just pissing in the wind.

VERNA: But—

MRS. GIBSON: I'll tell you something, Verna. My mother was a very ordinary woman. But she did something when I was a girl that I never forgot. She said, "You are free to make your own mistakes."

VERNA: Oh . . . . Well, that's fine, but why does Darcy always back Paul up? Why does she want to do everything his way?

EILEEN: Cut the crap, Verna. Darcy's like you in a lot of ways.

VERNA: Name one.

EILEEN: I can name you more than one. She's strong and capable. She's got solid principles, determination—

MRS. GIBSON: And she's a good kind person.

VERNA: I suppose she is.

MRS. GIBSON: Of course she is . . . . I know you're worried about the farm, but don't take it out on Darcy.

VERNA: You're damn right I'm worried. My God, we've got more debt today than we had ten years ago. Maybe Gibson left your place free and clear—

MRS. GIBSON: Now you hold on a moment.

EILEEN: Verna, shut up.

VERNA: Things are in a mess. Doesn't that scare you?

EILEEN: Of course it does.

VERNA: Well, then?

EILEEN: Well, don't just sit around moaning about it.

VERNA: I'm not moaning. Anyway, what are you doing about it?

EILEEN: I'll tell you what I'm doing . . . . I think I might go after the N.D.P. nomination in the next election. I've talked to a few people already.

VERNA: For God's sake. What a waste of time and energy.

EILEEN: Thanks for the vote of confidence.

VERNA: Do you really think that's gonna do the slightest bit of good?

EILEEN: How do I know? I have to try. And Verna—if Darcy and Greg want to start out farming, I'm gonna help them.

VERNA: Oh, is that what you're really here about? To talk about those two getting married?

EILEEN: Don't be ridiculous.

VERNA: A couple of stupid kids who haven't even finished high school?

EILEEN: They're not stupid.

VERNA: What would you call it? Darcy thinks all you have to do is love each other. Everything'll work out. Is that what you're promoting?

EILEEN: I'm not promoting anything.

VERNA: Maybe you're the one that's stupid.

EILEEN: Is that so? Blow it out your ear, Verna.

MRS. GIBSON: Verna. That was quite unworthy of you.

VERNA: Oh damn, I'm sorry.

EILEEN: I'm not stupid.

VERNA: I know you're not. I shouldn't have talked like that. I just get worried about the kids. Listen, Eileen. Darcy's almost finished grade eleven. When I read her school essays, I just about die, I'm so proud. Yes, she's good at farm work, but I want her to go on in school.

EILEEN: Yeah—but what does she want?

VERNA: She wants the farm—because that's all she's ever known.

EILEEN: She's old enough to decide.

VERNA: Like you were, I suppose. You could have gone to university. You could have been anything you wanted.

EILEEN: I wanted this.

VERNA: Didn't you ever—just for a moment—wonder what else you might have done?

EILEEN: All right. Maybe I did.

VERNA: Well?

EILEEN: You know damn well I had to help out on the farm after my dad died.

VERNA: What about your brothers?

EILEEN: They had jobs in town by then.

VERNA: Of course. And you couldn't expect them to give that up. So you gave up your future.

EILEEN: But I did want this.

VERNA: You'll never really know. (EILEEN *doesn't answer*) I just want Darcy to have a choice.

EILEEN: Like hell—you want her to have your choice.

VERNA: No. I want her to choose—but when she's ready.

EILEEN: She's ready now—and she's choosing Greg. And whatever they want to do, I'll back them. As long as my name's worth anything at the bank.

MRS. GIBSON: She's right, Verna. You'd do no less yourself.

VERNA: *(To* EILEEN*)* You're encouraging them.

EILEEN: I'm not.

VERNA: Yes, you are, and Darcy knows it. She's always telling me how smart you are. Eileen says this, Eileen does that.

EILEEN: Oh, for Pete's sake.

VERNA: You heard her. "Eileen knows what I mean." Oh, and I suppose she's going to help you run for the N.D.P. too. *(*EILEEN *doesn't answer)* She is! Isn't she?

EILEEN: She wants to work on my campaign.

VERNA: She's got more important things to worry about.

EILEEN: Like what?

VERNA: Like her future. Not some election everybody will have forgotten in a few months.

EILEEN: And you? You want her to leave the community she grew up in? Walk away from the biggest crisis we've ever faced?

VERNA: What in God's name can Darcy do?

EILEEN: What can anybody do?

VERNA: Isn't that my point?

EILEEN: Verna—

VERNA: You know what it means to start a farm these days. And you think it's fine for Darcy and Greg to get married.

EILEEN: I don't think it's "fine."

MRS. GIBSON: I think it's fine, Verna.

EILEEN: But I don't think it's wrong, either. And I don't tell Greg what to do, and neither did Larry.

VERNA: Will you wake up? You can't turn on the television without seeing farm auctions. Foreclosures. Farmers having to stand in line at the welfare office.

MRS. GIBSON: You're not a quitter, Verna.

VERNA: I look ahead, and you know what I see? Paul and me lined up with all the others. Mrs. Gibson, Paul can't do that. It's not in him.

EILEEN: Then you'll have to do it. If it comes to that. But it won't.

MRS. GIBSON: I know some who've had to do it.

VERNA: Sure—young families with kids. They have no choice.

EILEEN: It's not a handout, damn it. It's something they've earned a right to.

VERNA: N.D.P. talk. Paul's dad was a Liberal—as far as he's concerned, you don't take charity. He'd be a failure.

EILEEN: That's crazy. He can't control prices, and interest rates, and the cost of machinery. Well, can he?

VERNA: If we lose this place, none of that will matter. He'll be the one who lost the home place. After his mom and dad got through the Depression, and never gave up.

EILEEN: And we can't give up now . . . . Verna, this is more than a job to me. Way more.

VERNA: That's your problem.

EILEEN: I never saw it as a problem. I'm a Canadian, and I'm a farmer. Those are two things I don't throw away. Ever.

VERNA: What if there's no more next year country? What if it's over? I talked to Paul's sister last night—out near Swift Current. Their neighbour walked down to his barn . . . and shot himself. He couldn't figure out how to save the farm.

EILEEN: Paul would never do that.

VERNA: *(Starts to cry)* I'll tell you one thing, he's drinking a lot more than he used to.

EILEEN: All right, he's drinking more. But he wouldn't kill himself.

VERNA: Listen, when Paul gets up in the morning, he knows what he has to do. He knows the work, knows the shape of his day. What happens when he doesn't know any more?

MRS. GIBSON: Verna.

<h1 style="text-align:center">ACT TWO</h1>

VERNA, EILEEN, *and* MRS. GIBSON *stand as at the end of* ACT ONE, *as lights come up.*

UNCLE POMPILIU *enters down right and walks slowly up to the house. As he enters, the women turn to look at him. He comes in and lets the door slam. He looks tired and dispirited.*

POMPILIU: Oh my-my.

EILEEN: What's wrong?

POMPILIU: I don't feel well at all. I'm getting too old for this now.

MRS. GIBSON: Come and sit down.

POMPILIU *sits down at the table.*

EILEEN: I thought there was life in those old bones yet.

POMPILIU: There is, there is. They get weary all the same. Anyway, they don't need me. They got little girls down there working the same as men.

MRS. GIBSON: Never mind, my dear.

POMPILIU: I remember when I was little boy, down at the corral watching the branding . . . I got my own rope, and I'm practising roping fence posts . . . but I want to be in the corral, helping, because that's what men do.

MRS. GIBSON *sits down near him.*

POMPILIU: The sun beats down on my head . . . my face is hot, like I've got fever . . . there's men and horses all around, dust filling the air . . . .

They rope this one calf right in front of me, Jessie. He's so close . . . staring right at me . . . . The men come with branding iron . . . the calf is bawling and fighting to get away . . . and I smell the hair . . . burning . . . .

Then I see my *tata*—my dad—getting ready to castrate the calf .... I don't know why they do it, but I know it isn't something good.

I start to yell, and *tata* asks me what's wrong. I tell him he is hurting the calf ... I want him to stop. He says not to worry ... the calf is only scared ... because it's taken away from its mother ... he says the calves will find their mothers again soon ....

I run away to the house, but I still hear the calves ... my mama is there with the other women ... she's wearing a dark dress, and it's so hot in the kitchen .... I start to cry ... and she says, what's wrong, *draguts?*

I tell her about the calf ... she says, I know, it's sad, but it's what we have to do, it's our work ... and she gives me poppy seed cake, but I can't eat ....

Pretty soon I'm a bit older, and it's my work too ... and I do the work and I never say anything about it .... But the feelings never went away ... I see that now ... and I'm so tired ... I don't want to do it any more.

MRS. GIBSON *puts her hand on his shoulder.*

MRS. GIBSON: It's all right, my dear. You've done your share of the work.

POMPILIU: You know, Jessie, they say old people forget. I say it's a terrible thing to remember so well.

They are all quiet for a moment, then are startled by the sound of a car pulling up in the yard, spraying gravel.

VERNA: Now what?

VERNA *and* EILEEN *go to the window to look out.*

VERNA: No. Not today.

EILEEN: It's only Harvey Flint.

VERNA: He's coming to the house, for heaven's sake. *(To* EILEEN*)* Now don't you get arguing with him.

EILEEN: Okay, I won't.

UNCLE POMPILIU *gets up and goes to the cellar door.*

VERNA: Well, let's not stand here gawking . . . . Uncle Pompiliu —where are you going?

UNCLE POMPILIU *goes downstairs, not noticing the question.*

VERNA: What was I doing just now?

EILEEN: Verna—Relax.

VERNA: Everybody sit down.

EILEEN *and* MRS. GIBSON *sit at the table.* FLINT *knocks.* VERNA *answers. (*FLINT *wears a western suit, fancy cowboy boots.)*

VERNA: Mr. Flint. Hello. Won't you come in?

FLINT: Thanks, Mrs. Petrescu.

FLINT *enters, looks around, spots* EILEEN; *for a moment they just look at each other.*

FLINT: Well . . . Eileen.

EILEEN: Well . . . Harvey.

MRS. GIBSON: Hello, Mr. Flint.

FLINT: Hello, Mrs. Gibson. Hope you're well.

MRS. GIBSON: Very well, thank you.

VERNA: Sit down, Mr. Flint. I'll get you a coffee.

HARVEY *sits down.*

FLINT: Eileen . . . how's the flaming socialist? You're looking good.

EILEEN: Oh yeah? That's cause I live right.

FLINT: *(Laughs)* You never change, do you?

EILEEN: No, I haven't changed. I've had your number since high school.

FLINT: You were already a Red then, if I remember. (VERNA *brings coffee)* Thanks.

EILEEN: And you were a capitalist pig.

VERNA *looks annoyed.*

MRS. GIBSON: Now, Eileen, let the man drink his coffee.

FLINT: Mrs. Petrescu, I heard there was a roundup here today. Came by to see if I could lend a hand.

VERNA: Well, uh—

EILEEN: It's all over, Harvey. Supper's the only event left.

FLINT: Oh, that's too bad.

EILEEN: Guess you're a little out of touch, eh? I mean, you don't actually work twenty sections on your own, do you?

FLINT: Oh, no. My business in town takes most of my time.

VERNA: I imagine it must.

FLINT: I've got my farm computerized now though. All I have to do is punch in the co-ordinates for each quarter—and I get a print-out of what seed I used, what I sprayed with, how much—

EILEEN: I suppose you never even have to come in contact with actual dirt.

FLINT: Why should I? I have employees to do that for me.

VERNA: Mrs. Gibson, can I get you more coffee?

MRS. GIBSON: Not a thing, Verna.

VERNA: I heard in town you got yourself a new bull—Charolais was it?

FLINT: That's right. He's a beauty.

VERNA: I suppose that'll make a big difference to your herd over the years.

FLINT: Oh, it won't take that long. I started my own embryo transplant program. Just like those test-tube babies you read about.

VERNA: Uh, really . . . . How does it work?

FLINT: Easier than you'd think. You take your pure-bred cows and pump'em full of hormones. Makes'em super-ovulate.

MRS. GIBSON: Super-ovulate?

VERNA *gets up and resumes work.*

EILEEN: Sexy, eh? Each cow releases a whole bunch of eggs, and they fertilize them with the prize bull. Artificial insemination, of course. That way you don't waste a drop of semen.

MRS. GIBSON: Good heavens.

FLINT: You have a problem with that, Eileen?

EILEEN: Heck, no—it's the wave of the future. Course your pure-bred cows don't live all that long.

MRS. GIBSON: And . . . what happens next?

FLINT: We flush the embryos outta the cow's uterus. Sometimes we get twenty or thirty at a time.

MRS. GIBSON: I see. And then?

FLINT: I transplant them into my grade cows, and I get twenty or thirty pure-bred calves. In the same time it would've taken to get one the old way.

MRS. GIBSON: The old way.

FLINT: I can sell'em for two, three thousand apiece.

MRS. GIBSON: But Harvey, it's disgusting.

FLINT: No, it's just good business. Only way to get ahead these days.

MRS. GIBSON: If that's the way to get ahead nowadays, I'm glad Gibson's gone.

VERNA: *(To* HARVEY*)* More coffee?

FLINT: Oh . . . thank you.

VERNA *pours coffee.*

VERNA: Cream and sugar?

FLINT: No thanks. I can take things straight. Unlike our socialist friends. Eileen, I heard some ridiculous rumour you're after the N.D.P. nomination. Guess a few men might wanna throw their hats in, eh?

EILEEN: Maybe they don't want it as bad as I do.

FLINT: *(To* VERNA*)* Suppose your girl'll be a Red soon too.

VERNA: I beg your pardon?

FLINT: I mean, now she's going with Eileen's boy.

VERNA: Well, I guess you'd have to ask her, Mr. Flint. It's still a secret ballot in this country, you know.

FLINT: Of course, Mrs. Petrescu.

VERNA: We don't tell her how to vote.

FLINT: Of course not.

VERNA: For that matter, she isn't old enough to vote.

FLINT: Listen, I was just kidding you.

VERNA: You don't say.

UNCLE POMPILIU *enters from the cellar. At first he carries on as if he hasn't seen* FLINT.

POMPILIU: Ladies, have I got something special for you. Verna's own pickled peppers. Oh, we have a visitor. Why, it's Mr., uh, let me see, Mr.—

FLINT: Harvey Flint, Mr. Lupu. You remember me.

POMPILIU: Of course, of course. How are you, Harry?

FLINT: Harvey.

POMPILIU: We can eat them with bread and butter. Mr. Flitt can try some too.

VERNA: No, I don't think—

VERNA *looks at* FLINT *and changes her mind.*

Never mind.

She goes to get plates.

FLINT: That's Flint.

POMPILIU: What's that, sir?

FLINT: It's Flint. Harvey *Flint.* I, uh, just had my lunch not too long ago.

POMPILIU: Oh, no trouble at all, I assure you. See, the plates are all ready.

VERNA brings bread and butter and a couple of small plates. POMPILIU opens the jar of peppers.

POMPILIU: First, some bread and butter.

Butters some and holds it out to FLINT. When FLINT hesitates, he keeps it himself, tops it with a pepper.

POMPILIU: Ah, Verna! These are lovely.

He takes a big crunching bite, chews mightily.

Eileen, try some.

EILEEN helps herself to a piece of bread and a small pepper, and eats it with apparent pleasure.

EILEEN: Mmmm. Nice and crisp.

POMPILIU: *(Eating)* My God, that's good. Jessie, my dear. You try.

MRS. GIBSON takes a really big one and launches into it.

MRS. GIBSON: What a keen flavour. I wonder if we had these in Scotland.

POMPILIU: Without doubt, dear lady. This must be what they used to spice up the haggis. *(Big bite)*

VERNA reaches over and takes a pepper and begins to eat it. They all continue eating peppers.

Mr. Flatt, you're not eating.

They all look at FLINT. EILEEN bites into a pepper, giving FLINT a challenging look. He reaches tentatively for a pepper. He takes a big bite, chews.

Well?

FLINT: It's . . . well, it's . . . get me water! Aaaaagh!

VERNA *gets water.*

POMPILIU: You don't need water. Try a little bread.

VERNA *hands* FLINT *water.*

FLINT: *(Gulps water)* Thank you. *(Gulps more)* Oh, my God.

POMPILIU: I told you not to drink water.

FLINT: Oh my God!

POMPILIU: Why not eat a little bread?

FLINT: You old Romanian devil.

POMPILIU: What did you call me?

FLINT: Bread? Bread! *(Grabs some and eats)* Oh, Jesus. *(Eats some more)* If this damages my throat, Lupu—*(Eats more)* I'm gonna sue you for all you're worth.

POMPILIU: You'd try to take away a man's life savings?

FLINT: *(Eats bread)* You'll learn your lesson when I'm tooling around in your fancy sports car.

POMPILIU: The one pleasure of an old gentleman.

FLINT: Old gentleman? You're a Romanian son-of-a-bitch.

VERNA: Now just a blasted minute.

POMPILIU: That's it. I'm gonna sue *you,* Mr. Flint. I'll take away your two hundred thousand dollar tractor.

FLINT: Oh, for heaven's sake.

PAUL *is walking to the house as they argue.*

POMPILIU: You think Romanians aren't as good as other people?

FLINT: I didn't say that.

POMPILIU: You think we have no feelings? No religion?

FLINT: I didn't—

POMPILIU: You have insulted my people.

PAUL *enters the kitchen.*

PAUL: Hello, Flint.

POMPILIU: You have insulted my mother!

PAUL: He insulted Auntie Yulka?

FLINT: No.

MRS. GIBSON: It was just a little misunderstanding ... over some peppers.

PAUL: A little hot, were they? *(Sees peppers, takes bite)* Mmmmm, that really sets a guy up. Did you get some water, Flint?

FLINT: I don't need any goddamn water.

PAUL: Mr. Flint.

FLINT: I beg your pardon.

POMPILIU: *(Deliberately misunderstanding)* Oh, that's okay, Harley. I didn't realize you were so delicate.

PAUL: So, Flint ... anything I can help you with?

FLINT: I came by to lend a hand with the roundup . . . . And maybe have a little talk.

PAUL: If this is about that letter you sent with my fertilizer bill—

FLINT: What letter?

PAUL: I don't appreciate bein' threatened, Flint.

FLINT: What? ... Oh, that was just a form letter. All my overdue accounts get them.

VERNA: You know darn well you'll get paid the minute we have anything to pay you with.

FLINT: The computer prints those letters up automatically. It's nothing.

PAUL: I lost a hundred dollars on every cow I wintered last year.

VERNA: And we had to buy extra feed.

PAUL: And last summer I bought all that grasshopper poison from you, and whattaya know? Damn hoppers ate my wheat up anyway.

FLINT: Look, Petrescu, I didn't come here to talk about your fertilizer bill.

PAUL: You didn't?

FLINT: Why don't we step outside a moment—get a breath of fresh air.

PAUL: Okay. Sure.

They go out.

So what did you come here to talk about?

FLINT *hesitates.*

Say, you want to see Verna's garden?

PAUL *leads* FLINT *through the gate into the garden, stage left.*

EILEEN: My God, I thought my lips were gonna fall off.

MRS. GIBSON: Him and his artificial insemination.

POMPILIU: Too bad he can't find out what it's like for the bull.

MRS. GIBSON: Too bad he can't find out what it's like for the cow.

They laugh. Lights down on the kitchen, up on the garden.

FLINT: So—I guess you know, I've always liked this place.

PAUL: Oh?

FLINT: I know things have been tough the last few years. And I'm not trying to push, believe me. What I'm saying is, I'm prepared to make you a fair offer.

PAUL: A fair offer.

FLINT: In fact, I could do better than market value. This place would be a real improvement to my operation.

PAUL: Guess it would be.

FLINT: Good pastures, bottom land to grow feed. And a good spring, at least most years. Now, Ken Jackson's been talking to me about buying his place. And I could do that, but I really think this would be a better deal.

PAUL: Can't argue with you there.

FLINT: And if you wanted . . . . I'd be glad to have you stay on and work for me.

PAUL: Work for you. Flint, I've never worked for anybody else in my life. Unless you count my mom and dad.

FLINT: That'd be up to you, of course. I just mean, I know you're a good man with stock. That's worth something to me.

PAUL: You mean, just stay on here?

FLINT: Well, not exactly. Look, I had my lawyer come in . . . he wrote out a formal offer. Terms, disposition of stock, machinery, buildings, that kind of thing.

He takes a small envelope from his jacket pocket. Reluctantly, PAUL *takes it, puts it in his pocket.*

Take some time. Think it over.

PAUL: I don't have to tell you, Flint—selling's the last thing I want to do.

FLINT: Yeah, I know.

PAUL *and* HARVEY *return from the garden.* EILEEN *comes to the door and watches.*

I'd appreciate knowing soon, Petrescu.

PAUL: I'll tell you as soon as I know myself.

EILEEN *comes outside.*

I'm sorry, did you say you came to lend a hand?

FLINT: Uh, that's right, I did.

PAUL: We got a few calves left. Why don't you wander down to the corral?

FLINT: Oh . . . all right. I guess I could.

FLINT *heads for the corral, and* PAUL *enters the house.* EILEEN *calls to* FLINT.

EILEEN: Hang on, Harve, I'll show you how it's done.

FLINT *stops.*

FLINT: You? That's a laugh. Course, modesty was never one of your failings, was it?

EILEEN: Nope. I'm too honest a person.

FLINT: Why don't you stick to pots and pans? Or are you one of those types have to prove they can do anything a man can?

EILEEN: I don't have to prove anything. I admit there's a few things I can't do.

FLINT: Big of you.

EILEEN: Uh, sorry about the peppers.

FLINT: Yeah, well, I guess you people think I'm fair game.

EILEEN: You did get Verna mad with that crack about Darcy.

FLINT: I suppose I did . . . . So, how are things with you? We haven't talked in years. Your son must be halfway through high school.

EILEEN: Graduates this month.

FLINT: Is that a fact? Time moves on.

EILEEN: "A" average this year.

FLINT: Just like his old lady, eh?

EILEEN: Doesn't mean much to him though. He just wants to get started farming.

FLINT: If he's not prepared to use modern methods, there's not much point. Despite what you N.D.P. types think.

EILEEN: I'm not a type! And my differences with you go way beyond politics.

FLINT: I didn't think you ever got beyond politics.

EILEEN: Once in a while.

FLINT: Hell, you wouldn't even do the polka with me at the school dance when we were kids.

EILEEN: Oh sure—so you could have a good laugh at me? Look, Harve, I'm serious. I'm talking about the way you treat your land.

FLINT: I look after my land. You don't have to get all emotional about it.

EILEEN: You use more chemicals than anybody in this district.

FLINT: I do not.

EILEEN: Land is supposed to last. And I don't mean for just a few generations. Maybe if you had kids, you'd know what I'm talking about.

FLINT: If I had kids . . . . Look, I don't use any more chemicals than I have to. Just what it takes to get the job done.

EILEEN: Which job is that?

FLINT: Eileen, I'm the same as any other farmer. I'd like to help "feed the world," just like all the rest of them.

EILEEN: You're serious, aren't you?

FLINT: Sure I am.

EILEEN: Why not help them feed themselves? We should be growing less and building up our land.

FLINT: People aren't interested in growing less. Farmers will always try to improve their yields.

EILEEN: Sure. That's how we got the Sahara Desert.

FLINT: Oh, bull. You bleeding hearts moan about the land, but the fact is, you haven't got the initiative to learn how modern farming works.

EILEEN: Is that right?

FLINT: Yeah, that's right! . . . Look, I said I'd help at the corral, and I'm gonna do it.

EILEEN: Okay, let's go. We can always fight again later.

They start to move off.

FLINT: I can hardly wait.

EILEEN: I know.

They go off down right.

Lights up on the kitchen—on a tense silence between PAUL *and* VERNA, *with* MRS.GIBSON *and* POMPILIU *looking on.*

PAUL: Verna, what's eating you today?

VERNA: Today? Nothing in particular . . . today.

POMPILIU: Jessie, would you like to take a walk in the garden?

MRS. GIBSON: By all means, Mr. Lupu. We could carry on our little talk.

They head for the door.

POMPILIU: Our little talk, yes . . . . Let me show you Verna's gooseberries.

They go out.

MRS. GIBSON: Ah, gooseberries. Gooseberry jam on hot scones. I'll make that for you some time.

POMPILIU: I will live for the day, dear lady.

They go through the gate into the garden.

PAUL: Verna, you have been crabby as hell all day. And before that, all spring.

VERNA: Oh?

PAUL: And before that, all winter.

VERNA: Crabby?

PAUL: Mad, crabby, pissed off. Whatever you want to call it.

VERNA: You don't see any reason for me to be "pissed off"?

PAUL: I know things aren't that great with the farm, but I'm workin' on it as hard as I can.

VERNA: I didn't say you weren't.

PAUL goes to the fridge, opens a beer, and drinks. VERNA *looks annoyed. He sees it.*

PAUL: I suppose you're mad because I take the odd drink.

VERNA: It's not the *odd* drink I mind.

PAUL: It relaxes me. Takes my mind off my worries.

VERNA: Takes your mind off having to think—about yourself.

PAUL: Oh, really? *(Continues to drink)*

VERNA: Yes, really. About making a few changes.

PAUL: Is that so? Thirty years, and all of a sudden I'm not good enough any more.

VERNA: Some of your behaviour isn't.

PAUL: You think you got it tough? I could tell you about some guys—their wives would love to trade places with you.

VERNA: You mean because you don't beat me? There's more to life than not being a criminal.

PAUL: Verna, for God's sake. Are you trying to provoke me? Course I'm not a criminal.

VERNA: Yes, I am trying to provoke you—if that's what it takes.

PAUL: For Pete's sake, what do you want from me?

POMPILIU *and* MRS. GIBSON *enter from the garden (down left), stopping out of sight of* PAUL *and* VERNA.

VERNA: Tell me—what are we really doing out here?

PAUL: We're farming, Verna. This is our home.

VERNA: Maybe it's not my home. Not any more.

PAUL: Jesus.

PAUL *just looks at* VERNA *for a moment.*

PAUL: I'm going back to the corral. There must be something left to do.

POMPILIU *moves toward* PAUL.

POMPILIU: Hold on, Paul. I'll come with you.

PAUL: No need, Uncle Pompiliu. We're almost finished.

POMPILIU: Nevertheless, I will come. You need someone to give directions.

PAUL: All right, come on then. *(To* VERNA*)* Fifteen minutes should see the end of it.

PAUL *and* POMPILIU *head for the corral.*

MRS.GIBSON: Well. We'd better get on.

As VERNA *moves to go in, she sees a wild rose in* MRS. GIBSON'S *hair.*

VERNA: Mrs. Gibson, you've got a flower in your hair.

MRS. GIBSON: Yes, I suppose I do. Your uncle thought it would look nice.

VERNA: The old codger.

MRS. GIBSON: I may have encouraged him. Verna, I couldn't help noticing. You seem to be under . . . a bit of a strain.

VERNA: You could say that.

MRS. GIBSON: Isn't it bearable, my dear?

VERNA: I don't know. I'm getting so fed up with things.

MRS. GIBSON: With "things"?

VERNA: All right, with Paul. You work beside a man all your life, but you're always something less than him.

MRS. GIBSON: You should never allow yourself to be less.

VERNA: The place is getting to me too . . . . I don't know if I can keep living here.

MRS. GIBSON: Och, that's daft—you belong here.

VERNA: Is that right? So I suppose you belong in Scotland?

MRS. GIBSON: I remember nothing of Scotland now except poverty.

VERNA: But do you like what's here?

MRS. GIBSON: This is where I had my life with Gibson. Every place, every season, has some memory of that time.

VERNA: I used to love summer and making a garden. Now it just makes me hot and tired.

MRS. GIBSON: As if you never wanted to see another harvest? Never wanted to can one more jar of pickles?

VERNA: Yes! . . . But I thought you liked that stuff. I mean, that's how we all think of you. Jessie Gibson makes the best pickles, the best ketchup, the best chokecherry jelly.

MRS. GIBSON: Well, I do. Doesn't mean I have to love every minute.

VERNA: Oh.

MRS. GIBSON: I'm merely old, Verna. Not perfect.

VERNA: Sorry. I guess we fall into ways of looking at people.

MRS. GIBSON: Maybe we have to jolt people now and then.

VERNA: Make them really see you?

MRS. GIBSON: Something like that. Just don't expect miracles.

VERNA: Can't I just have a small miracle?

MRS. GIBSON: Best not to get your hopes up. (VERNA *laughs*) But try not to forget the good times, eh Verna? It's easy to do when you're mad.

VERNA: Is that what you do?

MRS. GIBSON: It's some of what I do. Like remembering haying time, when Gibson and I were young—the fine hot weather, the feeling that winter's as far away as it can get.

Gibson would be out mowing, and I'd jump in the old Plymouth and take him his dinner—roast beef sandwiches and buttermilk I kept down the well. I liked to watch him tip the sealer back and drink until his throat got too cold to stand it.

We'd lie on a blanket in the aspen bluff and hold each other, and we'd forget all about the hay. Just the two of us and the heat and the blue sky. That was when I loved this land . . . when I could feel it under our bodies and knew that it was alive too . . . .

VERNA: Listen, did you ever get really, really mad at Gibson? So you didn't know if you could ever forgive him?

MRS. GIBSON: Yes, and lots of times he felt the same way about me.

VERNA: Oh?

MRS. GIBSON: Verna . . . I didn't tell the truth before, about me and the teacher. There was something between us . . . for a time.

VERNA: Did Gibson know?

MRS. GIBSON: He saw Gabriel touch me, at the school field day. It looked innocent enough, but it wasn't. Then he knew, and it nearly broke us apart.

VERNA: It must have been terrible.

MRS. GIBSON: Yes, for a long time.

VERNA: Was this before or after those haying-time picnics?

MRS. GIBSON: Before.

VERNA: Really?

MRS. GIBSON: What I'd give to to have either of them back now.

VERNA: Jessie.

MRS. GIBSON: I tell you, age doesn't matter. It's hard to be alone. I still need a man to touch me.

VERNA: But I get so angry.

MRS. GIBSON: Yes.

VERNA: How do you get past it?

MRS. GIBSON: You don't bloody well get past it . . . Verna, if I had Gibson back alive again today, we'd still have fights.

VERNA: Jessie, I have to have something more in my life . . . I have to have something to go on.

MRS. GIBSON: Good. How do you plan to get it?

VERNA: I don't know. Paul shuts me out. I can't get through to him any more.

MRS. GIBSON: No?

VERNA: I don't think I can do it.

MRS. GIBSON: It does get harder when they're dead of course. You can say anything you want, but they hardly ever answer back. Takes a lot of the fun out of it.

VERNA: You still talk to Gibson?

MRS. GIBSON: I ask him why he went and died. I tell him it was damned inconsiderate. I wasn't through with Gibson, not by a long way. Imagine having a heart attack out in the field where I couldn't help him. What was he thinking of, I ask you?

VERNA *gives her a moment, then takes the chance to talk about another death.*

VERNA: If we hadn't been so far from town, Paul and I wouldn't have lost our first baby.

MRS. GIBSON: Probably not.

VERNA: When my baby died, I knew that nothing had ever really hurt me before and I knew I'd never see anything the same again.

MRS. GIBSON: No.

VERNA: It was ten years before I could face having another child ... maybe I shouldn't have waited so long ... I'd watch Darcy playing in the yard and I'd think of something awful that could happen. I'd run out to make sure she was all right. And she'd stop whatever she was doing and wait patiently till I went back in the house.

It was like fear was a plant that took root in me. A plant with those roots like tiny hairs ... that mix in with the soil till you can never separate them out again.

MRS. GIBSON: They say that losing a child is the worst sorrow. Of course I never had a child of my own, but I can believe it's true.

VERNA: You know, Jessie, when he died, I thought I'd never really be happy again.

MRS. GIBSON: And was that so?

VERNA: There were times I felt happy. But it wasn't the same. Something had hardened in me. Jessie, sometimes I wonder if it's right to enjoy anything.

MRS. GIBSON: You can't deny the bad things, Verna. But happiness is real too, and we shouldn't turn away from it.

VERNA: Why'd you tell me . . . about Gabriel?

MRS. GIBSON: I don't know. Perhaps I needed someone else to know. Besides, I'm tired of being the wise old woman.

VERNA: But you are wise.

MRS. GIBSON: Yes, well, you can't help but accumulate a bit of common sense along the way . . . but being old is a pain in many ways. The big thing I've noticed is the men stop asking you to dance.

They go into the house (lights down on the kitchen). EILEEN *and* FLINT *come on down right, tired but in a better humour,* HARVEY'S *fancy outfit a little the worse for wear.*

EILEEN: Okay, I admit it. You can still rope and tie a calf.

FLINT: Yeah, well, I guess you're not so bad yourself.

EILEEN: Now you just have to figure out how to let them go.

FLINT: Too bad you couldn't let a few things go, Eileen.

EILEEN: Me? You're the one that needs to let things go.

FLINT: Oh?

EILEEN: Like some of your modern methods, for instance.

FLINT: Will you give me a break? I was actually having fun there for a while.

EILEEN: It's your land that needs a break, Harve.

FLINT: Nothing wrong with how I treat my land.

EILEEN: You're only killing it, that's all.

FLINT: You can't kill land. It's a question of management.

EILEEN: I'll tell you one thing, Harvey. There was no dust bowl before white people came.

FLINT: Yeah, no development either. Hell, there was nothing here. Just buffalo everywhere, and a few thousand Indians.

EILEEN: A few thousand Indians who had worked out a way to live.

FLINT: But that way of life was goin' nowhere.

EILEEN: It was going on, and so was the land.

FLINT: So what do you think we should do? Organic farming?

EILEEN: Maybe. We've lost more than half the organic material in the soil. In less than a hundred years.

FLINT: You'd get more weeds than crop. Organic farming is a religion, not a way of farming.

EILEEN: Harvey, listen. There's a guy in the States who crossed wheat with wild grass.

FLINT: Wild grass? Come on.

EILEEN: He got a new kind of wheat. Drought and weed resistant— doesn't need a lot of chemicals. What if that could work?

FLINT: But we'd have to change everything we do. It'd be like starting all over.

EILEEN: Yes. That's what I'm saying.

FLINT: Look, Eileen, I guess you mean well, but you're a hopeless idealist.

EILEEN: You admit I'm an idealist.

There is almost a moment of closeness, then FLINT *backs away.*

FLINT: And if you think anybody's gonna vote for a bunch of radical garbage like that—

EILEEN: So what should they vote for? Bigger farms? More chemicals? Dead towns? I'll say this for you, Harvey—you haven't changed since high school either. You're just as pig-headed and callous and short-sighted as you were then.

FLINT: And you're the same sharp-tongued, ignorant, unfeminine, grade A bitch.

EILEEN: You're still jealous I beat you in every subject from algebra to motor mechanics.

FLINT: So how come I've got all the money?

EILEEN: You think that entitles you to own all the land around here?

FLINT: As much as I need and can afford. Yeah, I do.

EILEEN: How'd you get to be so greedy? When we were young, your family wasn't so different from everybody else.

FLINT: We were as poor as everybody else, if that's what you mean.

EILEEN: If you want to put it that way.

FLINT: Listen—you know what my dad left me when he died? A quarter section—that's what he came through the Depression with. A quarter section and an old Ford tractor and a house that was colder than a barn in winter. What I got since, I got by my own work. Summers I worked on the farm, winters I got a job in town.

EILEEN: Nobody says you don't work hard—

FLINT: My dad was pretty well wiped out by the Depression. I don't mean just money. I mean he never got over it. His spirit never came back. I'd see him around the place, and I could hardly stand to look at him.

EILEEN: That was a long time ago.

FLINT: Maybe. But when we buried him, I decided I was never gonna be like that. I wasn't gonna be a sitting duck for the banks or the government or anybody. I call my own shots. And anybody who gets in my way—well, he better look out for himself. That's what I decided, and that's the way I am.

EILEEN: Thanks for the warning. That's a pretty fancy explanation for thinking you deserve more than other people.

FLINT: Don't go thinking you're better than me.

EILEEN: I never said I was.

FLINT: You were thinking it. And while we're telling the truth here . . . .

EILEEN: No, wait . . . .

FLINT: I asked you to dance with me because I wanted to dance with you.

EILEEN: Did you really?

FLINT: What could be simpler, Eileen?

EILEEN: Nothing could ever be simple between us.

FLINT: No? I guess not.

EILEEN: We're in a war, Harvey. If your kind wins, we're heading for a countryside with no one living in it. Just giant combines, and big steel fences—marked "No Admittance."

FLINT: That's exactly where we've been heading . . . for the last twenty years.

EILEEN: Yeah? What are you gonna do when there's no towns left? No schools? No hospitals? No people? (FLINT *doesn't answer*) You think having money means you're right?

FLINT: It does. You're just afraid to admit it.

EILEEN: Afraid!

FLINT: You don't like the way things are—so you try to change them. Me, I accept things—if I have to, I change myself. I ride the cycles. Protect myself, so I can't be wiped out if I have a bad year . . . hell, five bad years.

EILEEN: What about the people who are being wiped out?

FLINT: If they can't hack it, the sooner they get out the better.

EILEEN: Like my husband, I suppose?

FLINT: Larry had a heart attack, didn't he?

EILEEN: Sure, and he also drank too much and smoked too much. Because no matter how hard he worked, he couldn't get the numbers to add up.

FLINT: I'm sorry about Larry.

EILEEN: It's this system we have. He couldn't make it work. It takes away a man's dignity, Harvey.

FLINT: I didn't make the system. I just try to live in it.

EILEEN: You're defending it. You like it.

FLINT: I'm sorry, I can't be any different. I have to be a realist.

They just look at each other. VERNA *comes out to the front step and sees them.*

I guess I'll go help them finish up.

EILEEN *watches* HARVEY *go back to the corral.*

After a moment she turns and walks to the house.

VERNA: At it again, eh? Don't you ever get tired of arguing about politics?

EILEEN: Damn you, Verna.

VERNA: What did you say?

EILEEN: You're nothing but a coward. A quitter.

VERNA: How dare you speak to me like that?

EILEEN: I dare all right.

VERNA: How can you stop Harvey's kind of farming? It's a world-wide system, for God's sake.

EILEEN: So?

VERNA: You think you can change that?

EILEEN: I don't know.

VERNA: You think anybody cares what you want?

EILEEN: I said, I don't know!

VERNA: I'm sorry . . . . But isn't it better to face it?

EILEEN: No, it's better to fight. I will go after that nomination. By God, I'm gonna make people listen.

VERNA: Fine. Do what you want.

EILEEN: Thanks a lot. I will.

VERNA: But you leave Darcy out of it.

EILEEN: You know damn well she wants to help. And you know damn well she wants to marry Greg.

VERNA: You *are* on her side.

EILEEN: Somebody has to be.

VERNA: You mind your own business. *(Suddenly remembers)* Oh, God—her cake.

VERNA and EILEEN run into the kitchen, where MRS. GIBSON is just taking the cake out.

MRS.GIBSON: Look, Verna—it's perfect.

VERNA: Well, if she thinks I'm icing it.

PAUL enters, down right (from corral). He opens the screen door and calls to VERNA.

PAUL: Verna, come outside a moment.

VERNA: Right now? We're almost ready for supper.

PAUL: I don't care about supper.

VERNA: Paul, for heaven's sake.

PAUL: Just come, all right?

VERNA: All right!

VERNA comes outside.

What is it?

PAUL: Are you really saying you don't wanna live here any more?

She doesn't answer.

Tell me why, Vern. I mean, you said you don't like my attitude. Well, what about you? You haven't been so easy to live with lately. Giving me the cold shoulder. Trying to run Darcy's life.

VERNA: I'm not.

PAUL: You think you got all the right on your side. Well, you don't. You just close your eyes to the truth.

VERNA; Is that so?

PAUL: Darcy and Greg wanna get married.

VERNA: They're not getting married, Paul. Not this summer.

PAUL: They wanna get married now, not when you think it's right. They got their minds made up.

VERNA: They can just unmake them.

PAUL: We could fix up the old folks' place for them.

VERNA: What? Nobody's lived there for ten years.

PAUL: It'd be nice having somebody living on the home place again. You always say it's lonely here.

VERNA: Don't you twist my words.

PAUL: Anyway, it's not in such bad shape. I had a look not too long ago.

VERNA: Paul, no. They've got nothing to live on, and no prospects of getting it.

PAUL: Didn't stop us.

VERNA: Things have changed since then. We don't even know if we'll be here next year.

PAUL: Where the hell else would we be?

VERNA: Farming doesn't work any more. It doesn't work for us, and it's not going to work for the children.

PAUL: Don't call them children. They can do anything we do.

VERNA: Sure, like all farm kids. They learn the job before they're old enough to think about it. If you took one generation of farm kids and raised them in town—that would be it for farming.

PAUL: Why would we do that? Farming's still a good life.

VERNA: No. We spend our lives raising food for city people, and they

don't know we exist. They think we're a bunch of hillbillies.

PAUL: I don't give a damn what city people think. Sure, things are tough. But we built this house ourselves. We've ridden over every acre of this land.

VERNA: So?

PAUL: I know you liked it too. You used to make me walk with you in the spring—to see the crocuses.

VERNA: Yes, I thought they were pretty. Now a field of crocuses just means a dry spring and poor pastures.

PAUL: It means the same as it did when we were young. You're the one that's changed. *(He gently turns her toward the hills)*

Verna, look. That line of hills? That's part of me. And the shape of that sky. I know that sky. I don't want another one. Look at it.

VERNA: I can't live here just for the sky. I'm sick of this life. Always fighting to get ahead . . . always ending up further behind. Having your hopes smashed too many times. Saying "next year" till the words turn bitter in your mouth.

PAUL: You think I've never felt that?

VERNA: I'm not twenty years old any more. I'm afraid.

PAUL: Well . . . I'm afraid too. Sometimes I'm scared as a little kid.

VERNA: Why didn't you tell me?

PAUL: I don't know.

VERNA: There has to be something between us . . . something we know for sure. Or I can't stand the bad things.

PAUL: I want to talk to you.

VERNA: You used to . . . . Look, it's time for supper.

PAUL: This is more important. Verna, you've been acting like I've done something you can't forgive. How can that be? I've never done anything so bad.

VERNA *hesitates.* DARCY *enters, down right.*

VERNA: Darcy, you are not getting married.

PAUL: Verna, she's been trying to tell you . . . she's gonna have a baby. That's why she doesn't want to wait.

VERNA: A baby.

PAUL: Now, Verna . . . .

VERNA: You did it on purpose.

DARCY: Mom, for God's sake.

VERNA: Damn it all. Damn it to hell.

PAUL: Verna, it'll be all right.

VERNA: You knew about this? You knew.

PAUL: No! Darcy just told me.

VERNA: *(To* DARCY*)* You'll throw it all away. Everything I wanted for you.

DARCY: I can't just do what you want.

VERNA: It's the oldest damn story in the world, isn't it? God, you must think I'm stupid.

DARCY: I don't think you're stupid.

VERNA: You did do it on purpose. Didn't you?

DARCY: Yes.

VERNA: Why, for God's sake? You could get married any time. You could have a baby any time. Darcy, you're so young.

DARCY: I'm not your baby any more, Verna.

VERNA: You don't know what you're doing.

DARCY: I do too.

VERNA: You'll have no life outside the farm—but you'll be treated as if you don't count at all.

DARCY: I'll be treated like a farmer.

VERNA: You won't be the farmer. You'll be the farmer's wife.

DARCY: I'll be the farmer and the farmer's wife.

VERNA: You're dreaming.

DARCY: You can't stop me.

VERNA: No.

PAUL: It'll work out. Maybe not like you planned, but it'll work out.

VERNA: I wanted you to have a chance for some dignity.

DARCY: I will.

PAUL: Damn it, Verna, she'll have that.

VERNA: Like I did, I suppose.

PAUL: I thought you did.

VERNA: Because you don't think. If something works for you, you think it must work for me too.

PAUL: What do you mean?

VERNA: I mean that a woman's contribution is not looked at the same way as a man's. Even if she's doing the same work. Are you telling me you don't know that?

PAUL: I don't think I do.

VERNA: Darcy, are you telling me you don't know? You know, all right.

DARCY *won't answer.*

VERNA: We're a little bit inferior. A little bit of a joke. Oh, look at Verna, she combined this whole great big wheat field all by herself.

PAUL: Verna, I've never said that.

VERNA: If we say something, it isn't noticed. If we do something, it must be easy. It must be less important. Like having a baby. Any fool could do that.

DARCY: Oh, for heaven's sake.

PAUL: I've never said that.

VERNA: Any fool could clean a house or look after kids. I mean, some city people think you should get paid for stuff like that. Can you imagine?

PAUL: Would you slow down. I can't keep up with this.

VERNA: Damn it, I will say this. I will figure it out. I have to make you see.

PAUL: I heard what you said, but damn it, it's just a way of talking. It doesn't mean anything.

VERNA: It does. It does mean something. It means we don't count for as much. The men don't think so, and after a while, neither do we.

PAUL: How can it matter that much?

VERNA: I don't know, but it does.

PAUL: Maybe it's been like you say, I don't know. But things are changing.

DARCY: That's right. It'll be different for me.

VERNA: No! You'll spend your life working as hard as any man—

DARCY: Mom—

VERNA: And never once will you hear it said that a woman is as good as a man.

PAUL: But that goes without saying.

VERNA: Does it? If it goes without saying, I'd like to hear you say it. Just once.

PAUL: All right. Women . . . .

VERNA *keeps looking at him.*

Women are just as good as men.

VERNA: My God. You said it.

PAUL: Sure I did. I couldn't have worked here all these years on my own. I know that. I . . . appreciate the work you've done.

VERNA *can't answer right away.*

Darcy, go on up to the house.

DARCY: What? Oh . . . all right.

DARCY *goes up to house.*

PAUL: Well? What are we gonna do?

VERNA: I don't know.

PAUL: I'm trying to understand what you're saying. I could try to be more like what you want. Maybe that's not enough any more, I don't know . . . I'd like to go on if you would.

VERNA: I'd like to be back where we used to be . . . a long time ago. Maybe there's no way back.

PAUL: How could we be like we were then? We lost a child. We raised a child. All the work we did . . . thirty years of it.

VERNA: You mean we're no longer the same people?

PAUL: I guess they're still there inside us. But we know more now. Those two people didn't know much about anything.

VERNA: So it's better to be middle-aged and beat-up like some old pickup truck?

PAUL: I don't know if it's better. It's just how it is.

VERNA: It took us thirty years to get to this. It doesn't seem like we got very far.

PAUL: Guess that depends where we were trying to go . . . . Vern, there's something else.

VERNA: What?

PAUL: Flint made me an offer.

VERNA: For our ranch? How much?

PAUL: Enough to buy a house in town and get by.

VERNA: My God, I didn't know anyone would want it.

PAUL: He wants it, all right. In fact, he'd hire me to help work the place. Just think—fifty years old, and my first regular job.

VERNA: You mean we could just stay on here? It might not be all that different. We could live pretty much the same.

PAUL: We'd have to live in town.

VERNA: Why couldn't we live here?

PAUL: He wouldn't be keeping the yard and buildings. It'd just be a few wheat fields and one big pasture.

VERNA: What about our house?

PAUL: Oh, he'd bulldoze and burn it. He don't need anyone living on the place.

VERNA: Why does he want it?

PAUL: It joins up to one corner of his land, and it's got a good spring, which he doesn't have. And then of course, it's *there*.

VERNA: What did you tell him?

PAUL: Told him we'd talk about it.

VERNA: You said that?

PAUL: Yeah. What did you think? That I wouldn't even talk to you?

VERNA: No . . . .

PAUL: He wants an answer pretty quick. If he doesn't get this, he's gonna bid on the Jacksons' place. I guess Jackson already approached him.

VERNA: So what's holding him back?

PAUL: Guess he'd rather have this.

VERNA: So you could live in town and work out here?

PAUL: Or look for some other kind of work.

VERNA: Like what?

PAUL: I don't know. What do you say, Vern? It's what you want, eh?

VERNA: You want me to answer right now?

PAUL: Flint's ready to deal.

VERNA: He'd take down the house? *(PAUL nods)* Dan and Trandafira's place too?

PAUL: Pretty well goes without saying.

VERNA: But you wanted the kids to live there.

PAUL: Yeah. But I gotta admit, this is probably the best offer we'd ever get . . . . Well?

VERNA: We could get clear of all that debt.

PAUL: Yeah.

VERNA: I wonder if anyone would notice . . . if we all just went away. If there was no one left on the land . . . just Harvey and his big machines.

PAUL: So you wanna take the offer?

VERNA *pauses.*

VERNA: No. I won't sell that man the farm.

PAUL: Okay, then.

VERNA: What about us?

PAUL: I know we might have to sell some time. I tried not to see it, but I know, all right. I even tried to think of other jobs I could do. I thought maybe I could be a welder or a trucker. If we could just try a couple more years. Then if it's not working, maybe we'd have to sell . . . I don't wanna leave this place. But I guess I won't die for it either.

Just think, we might end up being city people ourselves some day . . . I'm sorry it's been so hard. It's not what I hoped it would be.

VERNA: Nobody could have done more than you did.

PAUL: About Darcy. I wish they'd have waited too.

VERNA: Like they say, eh, "If you could be seventeen again, knowing what you know now."

PAUL: Forty-eight's not so old, you know.

VERNA: No.

PAUL: We're not finished yet, not by a long ways.

VERNA: Not finished with each other?

PAUL: No.

VERNA: We'll give it a try?

PAUL: Yeah . . . . See how it goes?

VERNA: Yeah.

> UNCLE POMPILIU *walks past them and enters the kitchen. Lights up on the kitchen where* EILEEN, DARCY, *and* MRS. GIBSON *are putting things on the table.*

POMPILIU: Just tell me supper's ready.

DARCY: Almost. Eileen, could you come with me for a moment?

EILEEN: What? Oh, sure.

> *They go out, through the door to the living-room (up left).*

POMPILIU: Jessie, I had too many winters on the farm. I want to rest now.

MRS.GIBSON: So what do we do? Forget it?

POMPILIU: Never. We can't forget it. At our age, Jessie . . . .

MRS.GIBSON: We'll work it out somehow. They exchange a glance, then hold each other and steal a kiss.

> *At the same time,* PAUL *and* VERNA *turn and walk to the house. They enter in time to see the kiss, just as* EILEEN *and* DARCY *enter by the up left door.*

> POMPILIU *and* MRS. GIBSON *continue kissing a moment longer, then slowly turn to look at the others.*

DARCY: I thought there was something going on.

PAUL: So what about it? You gonna have a summer wedding?

POMPILIU: Not exactly.

VERNA: Not *exactly?*

MRS. GIBSON: What he means is, we've sort of moved in together. For the summer.

POMPILIU: A wedding takes a lot out of you at our age. Besides, we wanted . . . .

MRS. GIBSON: We wanted to see how things worked out first.

PAUL: Well, I'm damned.

VERNA: Uncle Pompiliu . . . Jessie . . . Congratulations.

> VERNA *gives them each a hug.*

PAUL: Congratulations, Jessie. *(He kisses her)* Uncle Pompiliu, you old devil.

> PAUL *hugs* UNCLE POMPILIU. EILEEN *and* DARCY *get in on it too.*

MRS. GIBSON: We've still got a few things to work out.

POMPILIU: Jessie won't move to town. She says she can't leave her garden.

MRS. GIBSON: And he won't leave his place in Assiniboia. As if I could stand being cooped up there once the warm weather came.

POMPILIU: I won't spend another winter on the farm. Not even your farm.

MRS. GIBSON: Well, I'm not locking myself up in that cubby-hole you call an apartment.

POMPILIU: And I'm not going to be your hired hand. I'm too old.

MRS. GIBSON: Old! You're an old fool.

POMPILIU: Old fool, is it?

MRS. GIBSON: You heard me.

> *Everyone looks desperate for some way to stop the argument.*

EILEEN: Why don't you spend summers on the farm and winters in town in the apartment?

MRS. GIBSON: Summers . . .

POMPILIU: Winters . . .

They consider Eileen's suggestion, then nod as if thinking "It could work."

VERNA: Well, that's a relief.

DARCY: There will be a summer wedding though. Greg and I are getting married.

Everyone turns to VERNA.

VERNA: Well, don't all look at me. It wasn't my idea. But Darcy has made her choice.

MRS. GIBSON: Darcy.

PAUL: We're gonna fix up the old folks' place.

MRS. GIBSON: Good, I'll have more neighbours.

POMPILIU: We'll have a Romanian wedding. We'll feast for days—

DARCY: Okay!

POMPILIU: We'll drink red wine and plum brandy—

EILEEN: Let's get this supper on the road.

POMPILIU: And hurry, I'm losing strength fast. I'm not used to all this excitement.

EILEEN, DARCY, and MRS. GIBSON *move the last platters of food to the table.* VERNA *goes to the screen door and walks out to the space in front of the house and yells.*

VERNA: Supper, everybody! *(She listens, but hears nothing)* Come on, you guys.

There are muffled sounds from offstage: "All right!" "Coming!" "Hold your horses!"

PAUL *follows* VERNA *outside.*

PAUL: *(Yells)* Come on, you guys! Supper!

More answers from offstage, coming closer.

PAUL *moves a little closer to* VERNA.

PAUL: I hoped you wouldn't sell.

VERNA *turns towards* PAUL.

HARVEY FLINT *comes walking up from the corral, looking tired, his clothes rumpled and dusty.*

He stops when he sees PAUL *and* VERNA. *Nobody says anything, but he knows that for now,* PAUL *and* VERNA *aren't selling the farm.*

Looking at PAUL *and* VERNA, *he doesn't see where he's walking, and lands squarely in the cow pie.*

FLINT: Shit.

Blackout.

END OF PLAY

BARBARA SAPERGIA

Barbara Sapergia writes fiction and drama for stage, radio, television, and film. She has had seven professional stage productions, including *Roundup*, and is at work on a new play about Canadian silent film star Nell Shipman.

Sapergia has also written extensively for radio, and has recently completed a new work for CBC's Stereodrama. A television drama, *Any Farmers Left?*, was an earlier look at problems in the farming community. She has completed a filmscript, *Matty and Rose*, based on one of her stage plays. Her most recent book of fiction, *South Hill Girls*, was released in spring, 1992.

FLORENCE BEAN JAMES

In 1954 Florence Bean James rides six hours on a train. It is thirty degrees below zero. Mrs. James, at sixty-one, is ready to start a new career. She is going to coach an amateur drama group in rural Saskatchewan. The group, after a few sessions, has to stop rehearsals because of unusually warm weather. The actors have to drive their combines. The actors have to harvest grain.

"That was a waste," commented one Seattle artist reflecting on Florence's immigration to Canada and away from her famed Seattle Repertory Playhouse. Why a waste, I asked. Well, said the artist, Florence was capable of the most finished kind of theatre work. In Saskatchewan she was working with totally untrained people.

Mrs. James, however, did not consider her work in Saskatchewan a waste. She worked with amateur groups, professional groups, farmers' co-ops, United Church Women, Ken Mitchell, Jean Freeman, Shirley Douglas, Sue Kramer, Mary Ellen Burgess, Ken Kramer, W.O. Mitchell, and countless others. It is not an exaggeration to say that anyone in serious Saskatchewan theatre was either taught by Florence James or taught by somebody who was.

For Mrs. James Saskatchewan was not a waste because it provided an opportunity for what she called a "living" theatre, a theatre "by, for, and of the people." The United States would not permit her to make that contribution; during the Cold War she was blacklisted for politically relevant cultural activity. The unique living theatre that flourishes in Saskatchewan is arguably a result of our association with Florence Bean James.

She believed that you needed two things to succeed: talent and opportunity. Tommy Douglas's Co-operative Commonwealth Federation, the first socialist government in North America, had been elected in 1944. In 1948 the CCF had created the Saskatchewan Arts Board to give "the people of Saskatchewan the opportunity to participate in music, drama, visual arts, handicrafts, and other arts." This in a province without full electricity, bus service, or a decent auditorium in the capital city—in a country that did not yet have a Canada Council.

When she was past the age of sixty, Florence James was ready to grasp the new opportunity and pass it on to those with talent. She boarded trains that would take her to small-town Saskatchewan whenever a group asked. "I wasn't hired weather permitting." She stayed in hotels that did not have private bathrooms and fire escapes and worked with anyone who wanted to stage a play.

Florence said in one of her reports to the arts board during the fifties that she was "sowing seeds" and eventually there would be a "bumper harvest." Since that statement there have been lean and fat theatrical years, years of drought, depression, and abundant aesthetic richness.

The unique features of Saskatchewan theatre are reflected in the sense of artistic/social purpose passed on to us by Florence James. It is totally appropriate that Coteau Books should name this drama series for her. Florence understood that there could be no living theatre without writing, music, design, and performance growing out of the issues, the cultures, and the people of a region. Her kind of theatre spoke of history, labour, politics, racism, and deep human relationships. From her earliest teaching days at Fort San she encouraged and commissioned the playwrights of the region, because for her local writing was the foundation of a living, growing, rooted theatre.

The result of the opportunities Florence Bean James gave to us are evident in this series of scripts. It's a bumper harvest.

Rita Shelton Deverell
Toronto

DRAMA FROM COTEAU BOOKS

Other drama from Coteau Books is listed below. You may purchase or special order any of these titles from your favorite bookstore. For a complete catalogue of publications—fiction, poetry, drama, criticism, non-fiction and children's literature—please write to us at 401-2206 Dewdney Avenue, Regina, Saskatchewan S4R 1H3.

The Florence James Series

The Plainsman by Ken Mitchell. Set just before and after the 1885 North West Rebellion/Resistance, the two-act play features Gabriel and Madeleine Dumont. $7.95 (pbk) ISBN 1-55050-042-2

Roundup by Barbara Sapergia. This two-act play looks at the crisis in prairie agriculture along with a lively tale of love and marriage in three generations. $7.95 (pbk) ISBN 1-55050-41-4

Saskatoon Pie by Geoffrey Ursell. Set in Regina in 1906, this musical comedy deals with corruption, scandal, the CPR and women's suffrage. $7.95 (pbk) ISBN 1-55050-044-9

Talking Back by Don Kerr. Set against the colourful founding of the Co-operative Commonwealth Federation (CCF), the play is an engaging mix of historical drama, humour, and song. $7.95 (pbk) ISBN 1-55050-043-0

More Drama from Coteau Books

Black Powder by Rex Deverell. Music and lyrics by Geoffrey Ursell. This forceful and controversial play deals with the Bienfait and Estevan coal miners' strike of 1931. $5.00 (pbk) ISBN 0-919926-13-4

Studio One: Stories Made for Radio edited by Wayne Schmalz. An anthology of ten pieces written especially for radio by some of Canada's best writers including Lorna Crozier, Connie Gault, Patrick Lane, and Kim Morrissey. $9.95 (pbk) ISBN 1-55050-011-2